W9-BNO-082

Stadium Stories:

UCLA Bruins

Stadium Stories™ Series

Stadium Stories:

UCLA Bruins

Chris Roberts

INSIDERS' GUIDE®

GUILFORD, CONNECTICUT
AN IMPRINT OF THE GLOBE PEQUOT PRESS

To buy books in quantity for corporate use
or incentives, call **(800) 962–0973, ext. 4551,**
or e-mail **premiums@GlobePequot.com.**

INSIDERS' GUIDE®

Copyright © 2005 by The Globe Pequot Press

All rights reserved. No part of this book may be reproduced or transmitted in any form by any means, electronic or mechanical, including photocopying and recording, or by any information storage and retrieval system, except as may be expressly permitted by the 1976 Copyright Act or by the publisher. Requests for permission should be made in writing to The Globe Pequot Press, P.O. Box 480, Guilford, Connecticut 06437.

Insiders' Guide is a registered trademark of The Globe Pequot Press. Stadium Stories is a trademark of Morris Book Publishing, LLC.

Text design: Casey Shain

Cover photos: *front cover:* defense (Joe Robbins); *back cover:* top, coach Red Sanders and two players (AP/Wide World); bottom, coach with towel (Joe Robbins).

Library of Congress Cataloging-in-Publication Data
Roberts, Chris.
    Stadium stories : UCLA Bruins / Chris Roberts. — 1st ed.
      p. cm. — (Stadium stories series)
    ISBN 0-7627-3776-X
    1. University of California, Los Angeles—Football—History. 2. UCLA Bruins (Football team)—History. I. Title: UCLA Bruins. II. Title. III. Series.

GV958.U35R63 2005
796.332'63'0979494—dc22   2005046111

Manufactured in the United States of America
First Edition/First Printing

To the love of my life, Ann.

Also, the two things I'm most proud of, Dave and Nichole.

Contents

Acknowledgments

First I want to thank executive editor Mary Norris for the opportunity to put many of the past years' memories into print. In the beginning, when there were many doubts about putting the project on paper, there was nothing but encouragement from The Globe Pequot Press.

Also, this could not have taken place without the utmost support of the true UCLA Bruin fans and faithful who have been so supportive through the years. They have related stories that have been informative, fun, and exciting; and they have been there to share some of the biggest memories that this great university has provided. We have truly become friends over the years, and many of these golden moments were also shared with my family. And the Orange County Bruins, San Fernando Valley Bruins, Westside Bruins, South Bay Bruins, Orange County Alumni Association, and Santa Clarita Bruins are booster clubs of the UCLA program at its best.

The players and coaches have always been first class. There have been times spent behind the scenes with these people that are as precious as the wins.

Jim Gigliotti really helped in organizing the thoughts of text and was always very supportive. Jim, I really don't know what would have happened if you weren't there for me. Thank you.

Also, Mike and Ellen Urban of Urban Publishing Services helped in the final editing and structure of the stories and pictures. It has been a pleasure working with true professionals.

UCLA's sports information department is the best in the business. Marc Dellins runs it, and I know that even during the busy seasons, he has always helped me with a story or a quote or some statistics. His people, like Bill Bennett and Rich Bertoluci, have been tremendous. Thanks, gentlemen.

I also want to thank athletic director Dan Guerrero for his support. We talked right from the beginning, and he was always available for input. His entire staff in the athletic department has always been ready to help; this is what makes an endeavor like this so much fun. They are excited about the UCLA program, and believe me, it's contagious.

Introduction

The fall of 2005 will be my fourteenth year as the "Voice of the UCLA Bruins." There is nothing that makes me prouder. The wins have been fantastic. The losses are tough to take. This is a collection of stories about football at UCLA and the men that made those moments so memorable.

Now of course, I wasn't around at the beginning of this great university in the early 1900s, but researching the history of the school and digging into the archives has been nothing less than sensational. Talking with people who made that history and with those who watched it evolve has been rewarding. Delving into the past and learning how coaches from other eras schooled their players on the gridiron has truly been an education.

I have also witnessed a lot of what is covered in this book, both as a fan before coming on board and on the inside as the play-by-play man for UCLA.

One thing about being associated with a great tradition like UCLA is the supporters who have been there for years and the players and coaches who return and share their memories with you. I have talked about it with my broadcasting partners, who have played at UCLA. These Bruin fans love the former Bruin players and coaches. And even if certain coaches weren't loved when they were at the helm, none were forgotten, and sometimes they were even embraced in later years.

There have been lots of other books on UCLA football. This one is from a broadcaster's perspective. I love the history of this great institution. That is why some stories from the distant past are included. Others have occurred during just the past few years.

So enjoy it. I had a ball writing it and also living a good part of it!

The Early Years

With UCLA's relatively late start as an institution of higher learning, it is truly amazing that the school has come so far in such a short period of time. Now don't get me wrong, 1919 (the year UCLA was founded) *was* a long time ago in many ways—but not for a university that has achieved UCLA's level of distinction and success. Back in 1915 Edward Dickson, a University of California regent and the political editor of the *Los Angeles Express*, and Dr. Ernest Carroll Moore, the president of a two-year teacher's college called the Los Angeles State Normal School, located on Vermont Avenue in Los Angeles, had the idea of founding a new college in the Southern California area. By 1919 the two had convinced Governor William B. Stephens and the state legislature to make the Los Angeles State Normal School the Southern Branch of the Berkeley-based University of California.

As the years rolled along, the foundation for success was put in place. It took time, but it happened, and the school succeeded both academically and in intercollegiate athletics. Today, UCLA is one of the most respected campuses in the world.

In 1919 only 1,138 students attended the Southern Branch. And with a female to male student ratio of six-to-one, putting together a competitive football team was quite a challenge. Still, there was a team right from the beginning, thanks to Fred Cozens, the school's first head football coach and athletic director. One hundred men showed up for an open tryout for football in 1919. Cozens could never field more than nineteen players for practice or a game. That made scrimmaging against each other impossible. The team was behind the eight ball, then, from the start. Since the Berkeley campus team was known as the Bears, the branch team adopted the name "Cubs."

The Cubs were basically a freshman football team, and since there weren't many teams to play against in an era when baseball was king, most freshman teams at the time played against local high schools. The Cubs were no exception. The team's first game was against Manual Arts High School on October 3, 1919. As the *Los Angeles Times* put it, "The best that can be said for Coach

Name Game

The Bruins, original nickname was "Cubs," because its parent school, the University of California, was known as the Bears. "Cubs" is also the initials of Southern Branch of the University of California, spelled backward.

Cozens' team is that the men fought hard, but it was like a lightweight pugilist against a heavyweight. Not that the high school lads outweighed their opponents." The Cubs lost 74–0.

After losing three straight games, the Cubs got into the win column by defeating Occidental College at the team's first home game at Moore Field. The price of admission: 11 cents.

In the early years Moore Field was either hard as a rock or full of mud and straw and slippery as a catfish. It had rained all day before the game against Occidental, but 250 people attended the initial home encounter and saw their new school's football team win 7–2. Trailing 2–0 early in the fourth quarter on a muddy surface that produced one fumble after another, right half Abe Jacobsen recovered a loose ball and ran 60 yards for a touchdown. Red Banning kicked the extra point, and the Cubs soon made it official: They were winners!

The Cubs won the next week, too, beating Los Angeles Junior College 7–0. But that would be it. They would not win again in 1919. They would lose three in a row and finish their inaugural season with a 2–6 record.

That December the Cubs were invited to join the Southern California Intercollegiate Athletic Conference (SCIAC). It was tough going in the new league. The branch was just a two-year school, and the other teams in the conference had four-year programs and experienced football players. The Cubs began their years in the Southern Conference with a new coach, Harry Trotter, who would lead the team for the next three years.

During the school's early years, California was gaining national attention for its football in Berkeley. The Bears head coach was Andy Smith, who used what he called the Smith System—basically, it was to be in great shape and to punt, punt, and punt some more while waiting for a break. Lots of players transferred to Berkeley after finishing their two years at the branch, making the system the first, and maybe only, collegiate farm system in the United States. Smith had two freshman teams—his own in Berkeley and the one down south in Los Angeles. Did he recruit from the branch? You bet he did. The branch's change from a two- to a four-year college in 1924 meant the school could keep its students—including its football players—in Los Angeles for their entire college stay, instead of losing them in transfers to Berkeley.

In 1920 and 1921 the Cubs lost ten in a row. They dropped the first game of the 1920 season at Whittier, 103–0. (The next season Whittier won 62–0.) Trotter managed a couple of wins at the beginning of the 1922 season, then lost three of the next four, along with a tie, and that was it for his tenure. It was time for the Cubs to change head coaches again.

In 1923 James Cline was the new man in charge of the gridiron, but he didn't fare much better than Trotter, winning only two games in two years. By the end of 1924 it was time for him to go, too.

Around this time the team felt it should change its name from Cubs to something more football-like, so they became the Grizzlies. It sounded rough, tough, and scary—a force to be reckoned with—but it would be a while before the team lived up to its new name.

The school's football program began to command respect in 1925, with the arrival of William H. Spaulding. In fourteen seasons with the team, Spaulding elevated the football program to the next level. In fact Spaulding is probably one of the three most influential coaches in the team's history (the others being Red Sanders and Terry Donahue). In tribute to his legacy, Spaulding Field, where the Bruins practice to this day, bears this great man's name.

William Spaulding had already been a successful coach for eighteen years before coming out West to coach the Grizzlies. He had played fullback at Wabash College in Indiana and was a winner right from the start. During his senior year in 1905, Wabash beat Notre Dame in South Bend. It was the last time the Irish would lose at home until 1928.

When Spaulding graduated, he became the head coach at Western State Teachers College in Michigan, where he put in fifteen years as the school's football leader. Three of his teams there were undefeated. In 1922 he became the head coach at the University of Minnesota. In 1924, when his Gopher team played Illinois, he devised a game plan to halt the powerful running of the legendary Red Grange. Minnesota won 20–7, and Spaulding was a national sensation. He became known as "the man who stopped Red Grange."

Meanwhile out in Los Angeles, branch president Moore was looking for something different for his football program. He not only wanted to compete and to win, he also wanted national exposure. If his school was going to play football, he wanted to do it right. He wanted an experienced man to run the program, and William Spaulding was that man. Moore persuaded Spaulding to take over as the Grizzlies new head coach.

Spaulding had a pretty laid-back style. There were never any fiery speeches before games or at halftime. He didn't yell at players, and he spoke in a soft, but forceful, voice. Even during bad times, he tried to keep a sense of humor. And when his team suffered a defeat, he would encourage, not berate, his players. Some say Spaulding was too much of a gentleman, but don't tell that to the 1925 team.

Spaulding demanded his players be in tip-top shape. During the first practice of 1925, he had his players run wind sprint after wind sprint until they were ready to drop. When they headed for the showers thinking practice was over, Spaulding told them to take another lap around the track—and if they didn't make it, they could run three more!

The first team Spaulding coached was coming off a 0–5–3 record the season before he arrived. In his first game, against San Diego State, the Grizzlies won 7–0. Then they beat La Verne 16–3. They had never beaten their next opponent, Pomona, but this time they did, 26–0. The Grizzlies lost to Whittier 7–0 but bounced back to defeat Occidental 9–0, which at the time was a big upset. The branch was contending now for a conference title—from no wins a year earlier to four in Spaulding's first five games. The players loved it, and so did the student body. It wasn't long before some of the bigger-name schools wanted to put the Grizzlies on their schedule, and it was all because of Spaulding—not only because he was winning in Los Angeles, but also because of his reputation as a gunslinger from his Big Ten days.

Spaulding's team could handle the Southern Conference schools, but when the Grizzlies played some of the other teams — name-schools such as St. Mary's and Stanford — they just weren't ready. The Grizzlies finished that first year 5–3–1 for a second-place finish in the conference. The following season Spaulding's team finished 5–3 for another second-place finish.

During the 1926 season, the University of Montana Grizzlies filed a formal complaint against the branch for using the name "Grizzlies," and the young college was forced to come up with yet another new name. After weeks of searching, Berkeley offered the use of the name Bruin (Berkeley's teams were known both as Bears and Bruins). For the third time in eight seasons, the branch had a new nickname — and this one would stick.

Beginning February 1, 1927, the school would have a new name, too. It would no longer be called the Southern Branch. Instead, it officially became the University of California at Los Angeles, or UCLA. Just like "Bruins," UCLA was here to stay.

UCLA was busting at the seams in 1927 when the college broke ground for its new campus in Westwood. That same year the school's athletic department was invited to join the prestigious Pacific Coast Conference (PCC) — a move that signaled success for Spaulding.

UCLA officially joined the PCC in January of 1928. In the beginning the move proved too much for the Bruins. Although they had few problems with opponents outside of the PCC, they found it difficult to compete in conference. In particular the first two years playing crosstown rival USC were really rough. In 1929 the Bruins lost 76–0; the following year, it was 52–0.

Spaulding went on to coach through the 1938 season. In fourteen years he won seventy-two games — second-best to only

Road Trip

After beating USC late in the 1941 season, the Bruins still had one more game to play, at Florida. It was a long road trip by train. Because of the war and the troops coming west, the team sometimes had to stop along the way for other trains moving towards the Pacific. At one stop in El Paso, star halfback Bob Waterfield and some of his teammates went over the border to Juarez, only to be left behind, missing their connection.

The team was supposed to arrive four days before the game. Instead, all the players finally showed up the day before, arriving in Florida on different trains—just in time for the next day's contest, which UCLA won 30–27.

Terry Donahue in UCLA history. Spaulding's teams played .500 or better football in eleven seasons. His 1935 team tied for the PCC championship. And when the USC–UCLA rivalry resumed in 1936, his Bruins played the Trojans to a 7–7 tie.

Spaulding was proud of his players. Several men earned all-conference honors during his tenure, including end Leonard Wellendorf, center Homer Oliver, center Lee Coats, guard Verdi Boyer, halfback Chuck Cheshire, center Sherman Chavoor, and center John Ryland. More important, Spaulding put UCLA football on the national map. Other major powers in college football wanted to play the new upstart school on the West Coast.

Edwin "Babe" Horrell succeeded Spaulding in 1939 and coached at UCLA for the next six years. Horrell inherited a team that had Spaulding's fingerprints all over it and went 6–0–4 his

Star running back Cal Rossi (left) goes over figures with coach Bert LaBrucherie in 1945. AP/Wide World

Power Struggle

After World War II ended in 1945, UCLA's football squads for the next several seasons were made up of both war veterans and young kids. The veterans sometimes rebelled against the coaching staff's authority, making for a tough mix with young boys on the team just out of high school. This was the downfall of Coach LaBrucherie, and he was the first to admit it. His team in 1948 went 3–7. It was his last season.

first year. Horrell's first team included senior halfback Kenny Washington, who would become UCLA's first All-American, and end Woody Strode, who raced downfield to catch many of Washington's passes. There was also a young man on the scene named Jackie Robinson, who would later play baseball for the Brooklyn Dodgers and break major league baseball's color barrier.

Things took a turn for the worse in 1940, when the Bruins dropped to 1–9. Jackie Robinson was a one-man show, but he just wasn't enough. He was baseball bound, anyway.

In 1941 the Bruins and Trojans once again moved their annual match-up to the end of the season. On December 6, 1941, the schools played to a 7–7 tie. The next day, the Japanese attacked Pearl Harbor and put America in war mode. UCLA finished the season 5–5–1.

Even though Horrell's career won-lost record was 24–31–6, he coached the Bruins to a pair of firsts. In 1942 UCLA beat USC for the first time, 14–7, led by quarterback and future L. A. Ram Bob Waterfield, whose impressive numbers still rank him as

Coach LaBrucherie strategizes with players prior to the Rose Bowl game in January 1947. AP/Wide World

one of UCLA's all-time passing leaders. And after winning the PCC in 1942, the team made its first appearance in the Rose Bowl. Although they lost to Georgia 9–0 on New Year's Day, the Bruins had finally reached the "Granddaddy of Them All" and were very proud. Horrell coached two more years before giving way to Bert LaBrucherie in 1945.

After a modest start in his first season, when his team went 5–4, LaBrucherie coached the 1946 team to a 10–1 mark. The Bruins beat USC 13–7 and won the PCC before their lone loss came to Illinois in the Rose Bowl, 45–14. At the time, everyone thought LaBrucherie was the man—the coach for the foreseeable future. But just two years later, with two straight losses to USC and a losing year in 1948, he was out.

That's when "Red" arrived. And, oh, how things changed in Westwood when Mr. Sanders came on the scene.

The Red Sanders Show

The year 1954 is when it all came together for the Bruins. It's the year they won it all: nine straight games and UPI's national championship. "We were fortunate to have a fine group of young men who had a lot of ability, and we had a good schedule," says then-assistant coach Bill Barnes about the 1954 team. "It seemed that everything just fell into place." And UCLA's head coach in

1954 was a good one: Red Sanders. Red became a legend, and rightfully so, winning 77 percent of his games as the Bruins head man from 1949 to 1957 and leading his teams to three Pacific Coast Conference titles.

The national championship year of 1954 wasn't a one-year wonder, though. Red Sanders brought it along like a newborn babe. He got it underway in his first year at UCLA in 1949 and kept it going. It was something he created, nurtured, loved, and pampered in his own tough way. His players might laugh at that description, but the coach had his own way of doing things. He would stand for nothing less than perfection at practice. He was the first to say that you might play on Saturdays, but you win on Thursdays.

Sanders didn't just show up in Westwood and start winning, even though it might have seemed that way. He had paid his dues. Born in Asheville, North Carolina, and raised in Nashville, Tennessee, Sanders was a Southern boy all the way. He picked up the nickname "Red Bull" from his uncle, because he always wore a red sweater as a youngster. Later it was shortened to "Red," and it stuck.

Sanders played football and baseball during his college years at Vanderbilt. Though never a great athlete, Sanders was a student of the game. He loved the chess match on the field. His football coach, Dan McGuin, saw this tremendous talent and awareness and helped push young Red into a coaching career. McGuin would later say that Sanders had one of the best football brains he had ever seen.

Sanders was a winner from the beginning. He became a head coach on the prep level and, over an eight-year stretch, won fifty-

Coach Red Sanders poses with UCLA standouts (left to right) Ernie Stockert, Donn Moomaw, Paul Cameron, Ed Flynn, and Joe Sabol. AP/Wide World

five of sixty-one games. He got used to winning early in his career, and he liked it. He figured that if he was going to put in the hours of coaching and teaching young men, he might as well win, too. He was an assistant on the collegiate level at Clemson, Florida, and LSU before getting the head job at his alma mater, Vanderbilt, in 1940.

Sanders's first year at Vanderbilt was his only losing year as a college head coach. Then came World War II. When Red returned to Vanderbilt after serving three years as a commander in the Navy, his ball clubs got better and better. In 1948 his team was ranked twelfth in the country.

It was during this time that UCLA's athletic director, Wilbur Johns, was looking for a new head football coach. Legendary sportswriter Grantland Rice, who was friends with Sanders, told Johns about Sanders. Johns and Sanders soon crossed paths at an athletic convention in San Francisco, where they hit it off immediately. Johns offered the coach a contract, with a handshake they agreed, and the deal was done. Sanders would be the new football coach at UCLA for the 1949 season. (There is some disagreement as to whether Sanders had second thoughts about the move. Some say he did, and others say his word was his bond and he honored it. The bottom line is that he moved to California even after Vanderbilt offered him a lifetime contract. He was the new man in Westwood.)

Sanders knew the value of good assistants and brought his entire coaching staff with him to California. At Vanderbilt he had had a young assistant by the name of Paul "Bear" Bryant, who went on to become the legendary coach of Alabama's Crimson Tide. At UCLA Sanders had spectacular assistants who later became head coaches, too. Three of them eventually became head football coaches at UCLA: Tommy Prothro, Bill Barnes, and George Dickerson. (Another assistant, Jim Myers, would later be the head coach at Iowa and Texas A&M, and still later the offensive coordinator of the Dallas Cowboys.) The assistants were young and confident, just the way Sanders liked them. Barnes was in charge of scouting. The Bruins had a complete file on each team they played, and Barnes was on the road every

Watch What You Eat

There was never any love lost between the Bruins and Stanford in the 1950s. During one stay in Palo Alto in 1951, UCLA coach Red Sanders felt someone at the hotel where the Bruins were staying had purposely overfed his team. On the Friday night before the game, Sanders ordered New York steaks for his players, but the players were served huge two-inch-thick slabs of prime rib instead. The next day's pre-game meal was steak and potatoes. Sanders's team was slow and played a lethargic game against Stanford, losing 21–7. From then on UCLA players ate only fish on Fridays and a light meal before games on Saturdays. And in eight games from 1950 to 1957, UCLA beat Stanford six times. In the championship year of 1954, the Bruins defeated the Cardinal 72–0.

week to find out the tendencies of the Bruins next opponent. The only game he didn't miss was when UCLA played USC.

Sanders wanted the best for his ball club when he reported for duty in the spring of 1949. He wanted his team to play a 4–4 defense. "The ends would back off the line in passing situations and sometimes go out and cover a flanker back at a 10- to 15-yard level," says Barnes. "It was not man-to-man, but they were very much involved in the pass defense." Many pro and college teams would adapt to this defense. That was quite a compliment to Sanders.

Sanders changed a lot of things when he arrived at UCLA, from the color of the uniforms—the Bruin uniforms were dark blue, Sanders changed them to powder blue—to having the team break from the huddle in the "serpentine" style. To this day during homecoming games, the Bruins break from the huddle during the first possession in serpentine style: two rows of players face the quarterback, then snake out in a straight line up to the line of scrimmage.

One thing that didn't go over too well in the beginning, however, was Sanders's approach to offense: He installed the Single Wing to replace the T-formation. What was he doing installing an ancient offense in the modern T-formation era? Sanders knew he could confuse the defenses UCLA would face who were normally prepared for the latest modern offenses. Sanders utilized tailbacks who, in a split second, had to decide whether to run or throw, putting great pressure on linebackers and defensive backs. It was simple: They come up, you pass; they hang back, you run. It was what he knew best, and he felt he could win with it. Later on, when people complained after a win that his team wasn't very exciting, Sanders would say that losing was not fashionable, but winning was.

Red liked simplicity, a fact that was never more apparent than in the number-one principle of his football philosophy: "If you block and tackle better than your opponent, you win— period!" What a fundamental approach to football. It sounds easy, but it takes practice and hard work. Sanders's approach worked well with the young men of Westwood. There would be no whining—he wanted winning.

Nothing was ever taken for granted in preparing for the opposition. Sanders got his team new helmets and the latest in lightweight pads. His players would practice in heavy shoes, so that on game day they would feel light and quick. Sanders expected players to show up on time for practice and to always wear their helmets. He spoke like an army general, and hustle was the key word. "You better get a move on!" he would bark. There was never ever any walking. Once a player hit the field, he ran.

If a player had trouble holding on to the football or fumbled in a game, he had to "run the line"—a field-long formation of the squad, with the runner going through a human gauntlet of players trying to strip him of the ball. "That kind of cured the fumbling," says Barnes.

The Red Sanders era in Westwood began with a 6–3 record in 1949, the year Sanders was introduced to UCLA's crosstown rivalry with USC. Up until Sanders came to town, the Trojans never looked at the Bruins as much of a rival. In fact that first season USC won the game 21–7. A late touchdown by the Trojans to rub it in infuriated some of the Bruins and their coaching staff. It was something that Red would never forget. He wouldn't let his players let it go, either. The following year they beat the Trojans 39–0. The year after that, it was 21–7. After a loss in 1952, the Bruins came back with a solid 13–0 thumping. They didn't forget, and the early Sanders years made people sit up and take notice. The Bruins of the 1950s were for real.

Starting out with a 6–3 record as the new gridiron man in town made Sanders a hero in Westwood. Many people thought it would take him two or three years to build to that kind of mark.

Long Memory

Red Sanders hoped to build a relationship with sister school UC Berkeley when he arrived at UCLA as head coach in 1949. In 1950 Sanders asked "Pappy" Waldorf, the Bears head coach, if the Bruins could wear their powder blue home uniforms in Berkeley. In return, Red would let Cal wear its home uniforms in Los Angeles for future games. Waldorf was cold and brusque with Sanders, and refused the request. To add insult to injury, Cal won the game 35–0. It was the worst defeat Sanders had ever suffered, but he would never forget it. Never again would UCLA lose a game to Cal while Red was the head coach. He put an exclamation point on that vow with a 47–0 win over the Bears in 1955.

He had taken the Westwood talent, evaluated it, and installed a new look both offensively and defensively. It worked. A major part of his approach was that no one was bigger than the program. He wouldn't allow it. The team came first, and that was it.

In earlier years as a head coach in prep academy ball, Sanders had to recruit players. For every new prep to sign with his academy, he collected an extra $100. That experience helped on the college level. One of Sanders's prize recruits at UCLA was a young end out of Orange County named Donn Moomaw. Everyone thought this superb athlete would go to USC—in fact the Trojans even boasted about how Moomaw was USC material—

UCLA halfback John Hermann (33) flies through the air during the Bruins game against USC in 1953. AP/Wide World

but Sanders persuaded him to attend UCLA. Sanders would later shift Moomaw to linebacker, a move Moomaw initially thought of as a demotion. Moomaw, however, eventually became UCLA's first two-time All-American, and an award in his name is presented annually at the Bruins football banquet.

Sanders would put together another 6–3 season in 1950. Then he backed it up with a 5–3–1 mark in 1951. In 1952 the Bruins really came together at 8–1. Then came an 8–2 record in 1953, with the tough loss in the Rose Bowl setting the tone for the championship season.

Only two of the Bruins games in 1954 were close: a 12–7 victory over Maryland in the third game of the season and a narrow 21–20 victory at Washington one week later. UCLA won its other seven games by an average of 46 points. The Bruins routed Stanford (72–0), Oregon State (61–0), and Oregon (41–0). They capped their perfect season by blanking USC 34–0.

In all, the team scored 367 points and allowed only 40. The Bruins were ranked first in the country by UPI and second (to Ohio State) by the Associated Press.

UCLA's 1954 team set records like they were going out of style: points in a season (367), points in a game (72, against Stanford), touchdowns in a season (55), and scoring average (40.8 points per game, still number two all-time in school history).

In an era of players going both ways, Sanders put an emphasis on defense. "If you were good on defense, you were on the 'A' squad," Barnes says. "If not, you were on the 'B' team." On defense the Bruins allowed only 4.4 points per game, still the school record. UCLA's rushing defense (just 659 yards for the entire season) and total defense (1,708 yards) established records that still stand. "We spent more time on defense than offense," Barnes says. It paid off. All championship teams play great defense.

Fullback Bob Davenport (he was like "running into a car when you hit him," says Barnes), tailback Primo Villanueva, tackle Jack Ellena, and guard Jim Salsbury collected first-team All-American honors and were All-Coast and All-PCC selections. Guard Sam Boghosian was an Academic All-American and All-PCC choice.

Other key players on this team were All-Coast, All-PCC, and honorable mention All-Americans such as guard Hardiman Cureton, end and linebacker John Peterson, end Bob Heydenfeldt, wingback Jim Decker, tackle Joe Ray, end Rommie Loudd, and blocking back Terry Debay, a second-team Academic All-American. End Bob Long was a second-team All-Coast and All-PCC selection. Tackle Warner Benjamin and linebacker Gil Moreno were All-Coast honorable mention choices.

The rushing leaders that season were Decker (508 yards), Villanueva (486), and Davenport (479). Villanueva also passed for 400 yards and 5 touchdowns. Davenport scored 11 touchdowns. Sam Brown led the conference by averaging 26.2 yards per punt return. Heydenfeldt ranked second in the Pacific Coast Conference by averaging 39.9 yards per punt. Remember now, this was 1954. The numbers are different from what teams put up now. But the one thing this club did really well was win!

Perhaps the biggest hurdle for the 1954 team was Maryland. The Terrapins were the defending national champions and were coached by Jim Tatum, the national coach of the year in 1953.

Entering the game, Tatum felt he could outmuscle UCLA with Maryland's running from a sliding T-formation. But UCLA took advantage of Maryland turnovers early. One was a fumble on a punt snap that the Bruins recovered on the Terrapins 11 yard line. Bob Davenport eventually took it into the end zone for the first score of the game. The Bruins missed the conversion kick and went into halftime with a 6–0 lead.

Early in the fourth quarter, Maryland drove 63 yards to a touchdown and a 7–6 lead. Later in the period, a horrible punt

Perfect

Here's how UCLA forged its unbeaten season in 1954:

September 18	W	67	San Diego Naval Training Center	0
September 25	W	32	at Kansas	7
October 1	W	12	Maryland	7
October 9	W	21	at Washington	20
October 16	W	72	Stanford	0
October 23	W	61	at Oregon State	0
October 30	W	27	at California	6
November 6	W	41	Oregon	0
November 13	W	34	USC	0

that was shanked out of bounds gave the Bruins possession at the Terrapins 15 yard line. Villanueva and Davenport combined on two bruising runs, then Davenport scored from the 1 to win it for UCLA, 12–7. They had beaten the defending national champions. The Bruins didn't know it then, but they were heading to the top of the rankings themselves.

Another scare took place at Washington the following week. "Any time you played Washington, you could figure it was going to be a tough game," Barnes said. "Jim Owens was the coach up there, and Jim always had good teams. They always did a good job of recruiting and had a lot of big, tough guys." In the first half, UCLA led by 3 touchdowns, only to get careless and let the Huskies back in the game. Fumbles, missed tackles, and a listless second half took their toll on the Bruins. But Washington missed an extra point after its third touchdown, and UCLA hung on to win 21–20.

After the tough back-to-back games, some of the Bruins hit the injured list—John Hermann, Ray, Boghosian, Debay, and Decker—but all would return and no game was even close the remainder of the season.

Over the next three years Sanders posted winning records of 9–2, 7–3, and 8–2. In 1958 he passed away at the age of 53. He might be gone, but he will never be forgotten.

John Barnes: Rivalry Hero

Everybody has his or her own special memory of the annual Los Angeles city championship game between UCLA and USC. The great moments stretch back to 1929, when these teams first met. One thing about this traditional matchup is that no other rivalry has two big-time programs not only in the same city, but just a few miles apart.

It's a short jaunt down the 405 Freeway south to the 10 Freeway east to get from Westwood to USC.

The two schools may be close in distance, but there is no love lost between them. Fans align themselves with either the Bruins or the Trojans—and nothing in between. There have been people who have graduated from one school and did their graduate work at another. Still, they'll be the first to tell you, "I'm a Bruin," or "I'm definitely USC all the way," no matter where they finished their education.

One of the biggest names in the history of the UCLA–USC series was a relatively anonymous name on the Bruins depth chart at the beginning of the 1992 season. John Barnes, a player who started the year as the fifth-string quarterback, left his mark on the rivalry forever. Barnes's name sparks comments, conversations, and grand memories. This young man's story is one in a million, maybe one in ten million.

Barnes was born in Lewiston, Idaho. Lewiston is right next to Pullman, the home of Washington State University in eastern Washington. In fact it is so far east that most visiting teams stay at the only four-star hotel in the area, the University Inn in Moscow, Idaho.

When Barnes was a youngster his family moved to the Chicago area. That is where John got his first taste of playing quarterback, at St. Viator High School. He felt he impressed the coaches enough during his sophomore year that they were going to make him the starting quarterback the next season, his junior year. But the family moved again. John's dad was in the paper industry, buying and selling bulk paper for paper products and paperboard. Dad was getting a promotion, and this move would take the family to Southern California.

Quarterback John Barnes
played a key role in the
UCLA-USC game in 1992.
Otto Gruele Jr./Getty Images

So instead of being on the varsity at St. Viator, John Barnes lived in Orange County, where he attended Trabuco Hills High School. The school was in the same competitive league that included highly acclaimed quarterbacks such as Brett Johnson and Todd Marinovich, just a couple of the players who would go on to play at Division I colleges. Because of the move, John was late for football his junior year and did not play.

His senior year was another story. He did play, and he played well. But in a conference of tough competition, he felt left out in the shuffle because of Johnson and Marinovich, who had the big credentials coming into the season. Barnes was overlooked, maybe, but it did not squelch his desire to play college ball. He knew that somehow, some way, he was going to play Division I college football.

The Barnes football wagon's first stop was at Saddleback Junior College in Mission Viejo, California. Head coach Ken Swearingen had long been one of the area's top junior college coaches. To his credit, Barnes admits that he drove the coach nuts. He says he was, in his own words, a "little squirrelly." At first he was the starter, then he was benched. Things were not working out. The offensive coordinator, Bill Cunerty, talked with Barnes about making a change and getting away from Orange County. At that same time, Long Beach State called. It was the year that George Allen, the former Rams and Redskins coach from the NFL, was taking over the football program.

Barnes was excited. He went to a meeting the first day of practice and thought to himself, "This is the place for me." That feeling didn't last long. Whether it was a misunderstanding or whatever, he was told they didn't check out footballs to walk-ons. He played catch and warmed up with another quarterback, but at the end of the day he packed his bags and was gone. That was it—so much for Long Beach State.

John went back home, then headed to the Pacific Northwest. He went out for football at a small school called Western Oregon State College. As soon as he got there, he knew it was a mistake. He didn't get along with the offensive coordinator. In fact they disliked each other right from the beginning. He didn't start, and he felt he was wasting away not getting an opportunity. They tried him at tight end, but he really wanted to play quarterback. Time was running out on his eligibility.

Was Barnes being realistic? Was he a malcontent, a trouble-maker? He not only was running out of time, but he also was running out of colleges. Really, how many times can you transfer? And what about the real reason for going to college? There have been players in the past who have transferred themselves right out of an education. There have been situations where a young man chasing a dream has been in four different schools in five years. In his last year, he's a senior in terms of eligibility, but academically he's only a sophomore. Then, when his athletic career is over, sometimes he feels it's too much of a burden to continue in school and drops out, never to get his degree. Was this to be the path of John Barnes?

John got a call from one of his pals about going to the University of California at Santa Barbara. Why not? Things weren't working out at Western Oregon State. He would be a junior at Santa Barbara. It was his fourth school in four years, even if he never took any classes at one of them (Long Beach State).

At Santa Barbara, John finally found a home. Who wouldn't love the area? It is one of the best in the world, with beaches, greenery, and beautiful women. And the school is part of the

The Rivalry

Many college football fans believe that the UCLA–USC rivalry is the best in the country. The rivalry crosses every line imaginable—brothers, sisters, husband and wife, mother and daughter, best friends, neighbors, coworkers, it doesn't matter. When this big game happens in Los Angeles, everyone in the city takes sides.

Wagers are made and bets are placed. They aren't necessarily about money, though. You might have to wear the other school's jersey for a week if your team loses. Or cut off your hair, do special chores for your spouse, or mow your buddy's lawn for a month. Those are just a few of the promises made during the annual Bruin–Trojan week in the southland.

Oh, sure, there are some other huge games played across the country. Games such as Ohio State–Michigan, Auburn–Alabama, and Florida–Florida State, just to name a few. Even in the Pac-10, the conference has created a special rivalry week late in November with Stanford playing California, Washington playing Washington State, Arizona playing Arizona State, and Oregon playing Oregon State. In recent years, though, the Bruins and Trojans have moved their big game to December to accommodate the television networks. Here are just a handful of great moments in a great rivalry:

- The UCLA faithful remember Heisman Trophy–winner Gary Beban throwing a 52-yard, fourth-quarter touchdown pass to Kurt Altenberg with just 2:49 left in the 1965 game. It gave the Bruins a 20–16, come-from-behind win over the Trojans, and it sealed the conference championship and a trip to the Rose Bowl on New Year's Day.

- The next year senior quarterback Norman Dow made his first, and only, career start in place of the injured Beban against USC, which was unbeaten in conference play. Dow ran for 1 touchdown and set up another with a key run to lead UCLA to a 14–7 upset victory.

- The winningest coach in Pac-10 history, Terry Donahue, had his share of big Bruin wins. Two of those great victories against USC came in the 1980s. One came in 1980, when a pass from Jay Schroeder was tipped by a Trojan defender and grabbed by UCLA's Freeman McNeil, who scampered 58 yards for the winning touchdown with 2:07 left in a 20–17 win.

- In 1982 Donahue's defense made a great stop on the last play of the game to send the Bruins to the Rose Bowl. With no time left, USC scored a touchdown to pull within 1 point. But UCLA defensive lineman Karl Morgan sacked quarterback Scott Tinsley on the ensuing two-point conversion try, and the Bruins won a 20–19 thriller.

- In 1991 UCLA's 24–21 win over the Trojans started a record eight-game winning streak for the Bruins against their crosstown rival. There was only 1:12 left in the contest when linebacker Arnold Ale caused quarterback Reggie Perry to fumble. UCLA recovered the football to halt USC's comeback bid.

- Marvin Goodwin, one of UCLA's finest defensive backs, had a hand in sending the Bruins to the Rose Bowl in 1993, when he picked off a pass in the end zone to stop a driving USC team that was

(continued)

knocking on the Bruins door and ready to score. The final score: UCLA 27, USC 21. Goodwin's end-zone interception came with just 50 seconds left in the game.

- UCLA won a classic game in 1996. It was Bob Toledo's first year as the head coach, and the Bruins trailed USC by 17 points in the fourth quarter before rallying to tie the game. That sent the game into the new overtime format that is still used in college football today. Many fans had left the Rose Bowl midway through the fourth quarter and headed out to their cars for an early exit, only to listen to the Bruins comeback on the radio. They headed back into the stadium in droves. UCLA won 48–41 when Skip Hicks ran 25 yards for a touchdown in the second overtime, breaking tackles and rolling down the eastern sideline for what would be the winning score. It was officially over when Anthony Cobbs picked off a Trojan pass on USC's final possession. The game was, as the late legendary broadcaster Jim Healey would say, "a barn burner." It lasted four hours and twenty-three minutes, and it was unforgettable.

Quarterback Cade McNown slips past the USC defense in the 1996 game.

AP/Wide World

UC system, one of the tops in the nation for academics. Even more than that, Barnes found a coach who was not only looking for a quarterback, but also ran a one-back offense and would throw the ball forty or fifty times a game. Barnes and coach Rick Candaele hit it off immediately. The coach saw that the kid Barnes could throw. It was perfect timing.

When the press, media, and fans saw Barnes on the national stage after UCLA's 38–37 win over USC in 1992, it was like, "Where did he come from? He's an overnight success." They didn't realize that the year before, he had thrown for more than 2,500 yards and 25 touchdowns at Santa Barbara. In Candaele's offense, John was schooled not only in getting the ball into the end zone but also in winning. At Santa Barbara they were used to winning. Sure, they played San Francisco State, Chico State, Cal State Hayward, Humboldt, Azusa Pacific, Cal Lutheran, and the likes, but it was real football on the Division II level. In John's year there, the Gauchos went 7–3. Candalele was proud that Santa Barbara had winning seasons in each of his eight years as their head coach.

It was during that year of playing football at UCSB that Barnes went to his first UCLA–USC football game. Sitting in the stands that day, John thought, "This is what college football is all about." He didn't know how he was going to do it, but he wanted to be a part of major college football.

After the 1991 season, UC Santa Barbara dropped football. Lots of schools that had a hard time meeting their budgets had started to drop football. Cal State Fullerton, Long Beach State, and UCSB were eliminating the gridiron sport. Barnes had one year of eligibility left. He had heard that Bruins quarterback

Tommy Maddox had declared he was leaving UCLA for the NFL.

John had an idea while sitting on his couch at home. He knew he could play with the guys he saw at the UCLA–USC game. He was as good as they were. So he contacted Cunerty, his old offensive coordinator at Saddleback and a friend of Terry Donahue, UCLA's head coach, to see if he could set up an interview at UCLA. It worked. Barnes got the appointment.

Barnes looked every bit the part of the Southern California beach boy: long hair, bleached blond, tan. When he told his Mom that he was going to UCLA for an appointment, she said, "Well you better clean up and wear some good clothes."

John cut his hair, bought a new suit and tie, then packed some video from his Santa Barbara games into a briefcase and headed for Westwood. He walked onto Spaulding Field on the UCLA campus. The football team was holding practice at the end of the 1991 season in preparation for the John Hancock Bowl. When he walked onto the field and introduced himself to Donahue, he looked more like a stockbroker than a football player. The coach was shocked and said, "You're John Barnes, in a suit?" But Donahue was a classy guy, and he liked the look. Donahue decided he would at least let Barnes talk with Homer Smith, the offensive coordinator. Heck, it was better than a guy showing up in pair of cut-off jeans, needing a haircut, and wearing a pair of sandals—which is exactly how Barnes looked before the makeover!

Smith took the tapes into his little office near the practice field and closed the door, leaving Barnes on the field. He came out a few minutes later and walked over to John and said, "All right, come over here, I want you do some drops for me in front of the team." He wanted Barnes to simulate game conditions throwing the football, and he wanted to look at the young man's footwork. Barnes thought to himself, "You've got to be kidding me — in a full suit with dress shoes? It's slick out here without cleats on." But the young quarterback never let on what he was thinking. As Barnes went through the drills, Homer told him what he was doing wrong and what he was doing right.

At the end of the session, Homer leaned towards Donahue and said, "Well . . ." and let the word drag out for a period of time. Then Donahue did the same thing. His, "Well . . ." had the feeling of, "Thanks for coming out, we'll be in touch." But then Homer said, "You know, we could use another quarterback." Donahue, who trusted Homer's intuition and evaluation of talent, told Barnes, "Good. Come out in the spring." Barnes would be going to his fifth school. He would be a senior. He was a walk-on. But he was going to get a chance at UCLA.

When Barnes went to camp, he felt he could play as well as any other Bruins quarterback. But he was definitely the fifth quarterback, with Wayne Cook, Rob Walker, Ryan Fien, and Scott Fitterer all ahead of him. He never let being down at the bottom of the depth chart affect him, though. One thing about Barnes, he never lacked confidence. He was built like the other quarterbacks. He had good size, almost 6'3", and he weighed 225 pounds. He had a strong, accurate arm, and he had a decent touch on the ball. He wasn't fast, but he wasn't plodingly slow, either. He felt that under Smith's tutelage, he'd become quicker.

Cook blew out his knee in the first game of the year, against Cal State Fullerton. Walker then got his chance. He hurt his ankle after helping the Bruins to wins over the Titans, BYU, and San Diego State.

The Bruins would lose the next two games, one at Arizona and another against Stanford at the Rose Bowl. With both Cook and Walker out, the competition was between the true freshman Fien and the senior transfer Barnes (UCLA had decided to red-shirt Fitterer).

Going into the Washington State game in Pullman, Donahue decided to go with Barnes. At a fireside-type chat with the team, the coach invited players to speak up. Barnes, whom teammates were just getting to know, spoke up. He started talking about the Vietnam War, the opposition (the Cougars), friendly fire, attacking, taking over in enemy territory—using combat terms for football. The team got fired up. They were ready, or so they thought.

Donahue later told Barnes, "How could I not start a guy who talks about Hamburger Hill [one of the great battles of the Vietnam War] and UCLA football?" Donahue was also a great motivator, getting players ready for big games with any anecdote he could use to pump them up.

But Barnes was eventually pulled from the Washington State game, after throwing an interception that was run back for a touchdown by Marcus Fields. Fien finished up the contest as UCLA lost 30–17.

After the game, just miles from where he was born in Lewiston, Idaho, Barnes was in tears as he visited with his family. He had his chance, and he felt he blew it. His mom wanted him to

Improvisation

The Bruins didn't know that quarterback John Barnes suffered from dyslexia. He had some major problems learning the offense and verbalizing in the huddle.

At the California game in 1992, UCLA had changed the offense completely, with one running back and two tight ends. John told quarterbacks coach Rick Neuheisel that he couldn't remember the plays, the blocking schemes, or to whom he should throw.

"Here's what we're going to do," Neuheisel said. "When our primary receiver is the X man, I'll give you the [X] sign from the sidelines. And when the primary receiver is Y, I'll give you the sign like the rock group Village People [who sang "YMCA"]. I'll signal Y with my arms."

come home and not fly back with the team to Los Angeles. But there was something inside of John that made him say no. He was going back with the Bruins to face the loss like a man.

When John got on the plane, he sat with quarterbacks coach Rick Neuheisel all the way back to Southern California. Neuheisel talked about opportunities, and how you have to capitalize on them when they come. The assistant coach knew what he was talking about. He was a former walk-on. He had had an opportunity or two in his career and failed. But he was also very successful. He was the MVP of the 1984 Rose Bowl, when he threw for 298 yards and 4 touchdowns to lead the Bruins past fourth-ranked Illinois 45–9.

It was so uplifting for Barnes to sit next to Neuheisel that he couldn't wait for practice the following week. The Bruins were in the midst of a five-game losing streak. But Barnes worked hard while waiting for his next chance.

Donahue used to say, "We need to make plays." He would use that phrase when backups would get a chance to play after injuries. The Bruins stopped the five-game skid by beating Oregon State 26–14 in their ninth game. Then they defeated Oregon 9–6 in Eugene on a field goal late in the game by Luis Perez. Barnes, who replaced the starter Walker (who had recovered from his ankle sprain), led the team on a drive to the big field goal.

John was earning the respect of his teammates. Standout lineman Craig Novitsky told Barnes that he was his quarterback, and that the men up front would take care of him. And did Barnes have a terrific front line: Novitsky, Vaughn Parker, Aaron Gidion, Ron Neilson, and Jonathan Ogden. Now, on to the final game and USC.

Donahue announced that Barnes would start against the heavily favored Trojans. Donahue did a great job of not letting his senior walk-on get caught up in the pre-game hype. And maybe, just maybe, Barnes was still a little too naive to really understand how big this rivalry was.

UCLA trailed the Trojans 31–17 in the fourth quarter before going to work. Barnes led the Bruins on a 69-yard drive and finished it off with a 29-yard touchdown pass to J. J. Stokes. Then it was an 80-yard drive by Barnes, with two huge pass plays totaling 73 yards, Stokes again being the big receiver. Kevin Williams ran in for the tying score from one yard out with 7 minutes left to play.

Fame Is Fleeting

After UCLA's big win over USC in 1992, Bruins quarterback John Barnes and his girlfriend stopped at a gas and convenience store in Pasadena. His girlfriend went into the store. Just then a big white Mercedes pulled up and a well-dressed man, who had just been to the game, jumped out and told Barnes, "Put fifteen dollars in from pump one."

John's girlfriend came out of the store and saw him pumping gas. "What are you doing?" she asked. "This guy just came from the game and asked me to get him some gas," he said. "So I'm doing it." The man in the Mercedes didn't know Barnes from Adam!

UCLA's defense forced USC to go three and out. After the punt the Bruins took over on their own 4 yard line. Two runs and 6 yards made it third-and-4 from the 10. Barnes dropped back to pass and hit Stokes again. J. J. made a terrific run after the catch and took it 90 yards for a touchdown. Now the Bruins led 38–31 with 3:08 to play.

USC quarterback Rob Johnson drove his team 69 yards to a touchdown in the closing seconds. The Trojans went for a two-point conversion. But Johnson's pass in the left corner of the end zone was knocked away by UCLA linebacker Nkosi Littleton, and the Bruins won 38–37.

Barnes finished his collegiate career with 385 yards passing (263 to Stokes) in his biggest game. He passed for 2 touchdowns and guided a huge win at the Rose Bowl over USC. It is truly an incredible story of a young man who never quit chasing his dream.

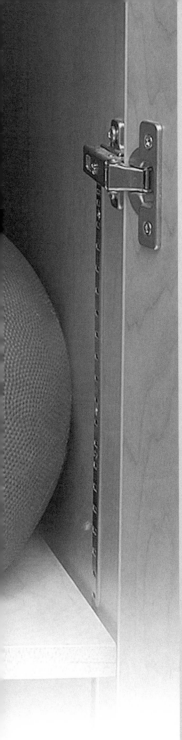

Best of the Best: Gary Beban

UCLA athletes have won their share of honors over the years. There have been All-American selections, all-conference picks, and numerous other award winners as well. But while each award is prestigious in its own right, the best of the best is the Heisman Trophy, presented annually to the best college football player in the nation.

UCLA football players have earned serious consideration for the Heisman twenty times since the award was established in 1935. End Burr Baldwin was the first in 1946, when he finished seventh in the voting. Half-back Paul Cameron had a shot at the trophy twice: In 1952 he ended up sixth on the list, and in 1953 he was third. Linebacker Donn Moomaw was fourth in the balloting in 1952.

Jack Ellena, a tackle from UCLA's national championship team, finished seventh in the 1954 balloting. Billy Kilmer, a half-back for the Bruins (we remember him as a quarterback, especially in the pros), collected enough votes to finish fifth in 1960. Running back Mel Farr (seventh in 1966), running back Kermit Johnson (seventh in 1973), quarterback Jeff Dankworth (tenth in 1976), linebacker Jerry Robinson (tenth in 1978), safety Kenny Easley (ninth in 1980), running back Gaston Green (eighth in 1987), and wide receiver J. J. Stokes (seventh in 1993) also placed in the top ten. The other Bruins who finished high in the balloting were quarterbacks: Tom Ramsey in 1982 (seventh), Troy Aikman in 1988 (third), and Cade McNown in 1997 (eighth) and 1998 (third).

But only one Bruin is included in the pantheon of college football greats whose names are on the Heisman Trophy: quarterback Gary Beban, who finished fourth as a junior in 1966 before winning the award in 1967, his senior year.

Beban played his prep football at Sequoia High School in Redwood City, California. Sequoia had a winning tradition that would have a major impact on Beban for the rest of his playing days. Joe Marvin was the head coach when Gary started his high school career. Not only was Marvin a former Bruin (he was a back from 1949 to 1951), he also was a tremendous high school coach whose teams won twenty-nine straight games playing out

Quarterback Gary Beban scampers for 27 yards against Michigan State in 1966. *AP/Wide World*

of the Single Wing. Beban started playing football as a junior at Sequoia and helped extend that streak to thirty-four in a row before a loss. The defeat was hard to take, but it insured that Beban would never take future games, whether in high school or college, for granted.

In the early 1960s, baseball was the number-one sport in the Bay Area. The Giants had come west from the Polo Grounds in New York in 1958, and San Francisco welcomed major league baseball much like Los Angeles, which went crazy about the Dodgers when they moved from Brooklyn to Chavez Ravine.

Even before he entered high school, Beban was a shortstop with a great arm and good range up the middle on a baseball diamond. The kid was an athlete, and baseball was his first love. Beban figured he would play baseball and a little basketball in high school, and then more baseball in the summer. Hey, this was Willie Mays country and the home of Willie McCovey, Orlando Cepeda, Felipe Alou, Juan Marichal, and Jimmy Davenport. Every kid wanted to put on a Giants uniform when he grew up.

After his sophomore year in high school, Gary was told that if he wanted to play baseball, he would have to play football, also. The head football coach was a buddy of the baseball coach, and they wanted to share Beban's athletic skills. Gary got the message loud and clear and went out for football his junior year. That's how he started on the gridiron.

At the end of his high school career, Beban needed to decide between baseball and football—between the "D" leagues in the Pittsburgh Pirates organization or going to UCLA for four years to play with the Bruins. He made up his mind in March 1964, while on a recruiting trip to UCLA, when he caught sight of the first of John Wooden's ten national-championship basketball teams arriving back in Los Angeles after defeating Duke in the title game. When Gary looked at Gail Goodrich, Walt Hazzard, Keith Erickson, Fred Slaughter, and Jack Hirsch, he thought, "These guys are athletes just like me, and they are national champions. I want that, too." At that moment, the decision was made. College football was for him.

Back in the early 1960s, the rules about visiting campuses weren't as strict as they are now, and Beban took every opportunity to visit UCLA while being recruited by head coach Bill Barnes. He spent a lot of time with Dick Mansperger, one of Barnes's assistants, who tried to persuade the young Beban that the Bruins were the way to go. Beban loved Westwood, but Cal (California) was interested in him, too. "Players from northern California loved to go south and attend school," Beban says, "and players from the southern part of the state were inclined to travel north. The ones who were confused went to Santa Barbara."

The summer before he came to UCLA, Beban worked with a junior-college coach named Dick Vermeil (a future UCLA head coach) on taking snaps from center and how to play the quarterback position. In high school Beban had been a Single Wing tailback and had never taken a snap from under center. The extra work proved invaluable when Gary went to Westwood.

Back in those days, freshmen weren't allowed to play varsity. And in 1964 Beban's team played only three freshman games while practicing with the big guys daily. Gary was a little nervous as a freshman, which was only natural. On his first day of practice, he got clobbered during a scrimmage. Ducky Drake, the trainer for whom the on-campus track stadium is named, told Beban, "Given your size, you won't be here long." Gary was 6' 1", but he weighed only 167 pounds.

The biggest adjustments for any young man entering Division I football are the speed of the game, the ferocity of the hitting, and the quickness of the players. Beban wasn't ready for all that. But being a student of the game, and with tons of hard work, he adapted. Gary had never lifted weights until going to Westwood. And he had never worked on his running until he met with UCLA's Jim Bush, arguably the best track coach ever. The intensity of those drills paid off—he was slowly but surely getting ready for his sophomore year. By the spring of 1965, he had gained thirty pounds and felt stronger and quicker than ever before.

What happened on January 1, 1965, would shape the rest of Beban's career at UCLA: Oregon State's Tommy Prothro, Beban's favorite coach during the recruiting process, was named the Bruins new head coach. "If you talked with any player from 1965 to 1969, they will tell you the football program wouldn't have been what it was without Prothro at the helm during those years," Beban says. In five seasons under Prothro, the Bruins would never win fewer than seven games a year. They won the 1966 Rose Bowl, and they were ranked fourth in the polls in 1965, fifth in 1966, and tenth in 1967 and 1969.

Beban chuckled to himself knowing that Prothro would be calling the shots. Gary liked the quarterback-friendly offense Oregon State had run during Prothro's reign there. Terry Baker, a quarterback, won the Heisman Trophy while with the Beavers. A quarterback who could play Prothro's offense would be nationally recognized. But Beban thought there was no way he could be a starter in his sophomore year with a new head coach in town. Or could he?

Prothro's offense was quarterback driven. He had to have a player who could pass and also run the ball. It really was a modified Single Wing approach, which Beban had studied even before Prothro's arrival.

In Prothro's scheme, the quarterback worked the winged-T with quickness. He had to take a half step before the ball was snapped, enabling him to get out around the corner. Timing on the snap between the center and quarterback had to be perfect. Every play was like an option pass or run. If the quarterback read a linebacker coming up, he would throw. If the defense held back, he would run. That's how Prothro's quarterbacks could accumulate so much total offense.

Beban felt like the Bruin seniors in 1965 came through in some important areas. His center was Morris "Bo" Freedman. Together they consistently worked on the center snap. When he rolled out, Beban had three experienced pass catchers in receivers Dick Witcher and Kurt Altenberg, and tight end Byron Nelson. In the backfield, veteran fullback Paul Hourgan and running back Mel Farr were weapons, too. They could run or turn into receivers or blockers. It looked as if Beban fit in perfectly with Prothro's game plan. He was going to be the starting sophomore quarterback.

Another sophomore on the 1965 Bruins who played defense and was a youthful, take-charge guy was All-American linebacker Don Manning. He might have been young, but he let his play, and his voice, be heard. Junior defensive lineman John Richard-

An Athlete and a Scholar

Gary Beban won numerous national awards during his UCLA career. In 1967, in addition to winning the Heisman Trophy, he won the Maxwell Award as the player of the year and was named the Columbus Touchdown Club Player of the Year and the Washington D. C. Touchdown Club Player of the Year. He was also a unanimous All-American selection and a first-team All-AAWU choice. Beban's proudest achievement was his selection as the National Football Foundation's Scholar-Athlete of the Year for 1967. The award meant so much to him because it epitomized the meaning of going to college and playing football.

son was another team leader. He weighed 254 pounds, which was huge for that era. The year before, Richardson played both sides of the ball. The players loved the big man and listened to his positive motivation. Prothro made him stick to defense in 1965, and he became an All-American.

The 1965 sophomore class came up with a slogan: "We are not going to lose on California soil." And they didn't. By the end of the 1965 season, many college football observers considered UCLA's team the best in the nation.

The 1965 season included tough road games at Michigan State, Penn State, Missouri, and Tennessee. The Bruins lost the opening game at Michigan State 13–3. The hitting was harder than anyone imagined. The Spartans were good blockers and tacklers and had speed. Gary later told his dad that if all the games were going to be like that, "It could be a long season." UCLA had just played one of the best teams in the nation on the road, and lost. It was a rough way to start.

After the game, Prothro said something that impressed Beban. "We underestimated Michigan State," he told the players. "We didn't prepare or coach you properly for this game. You played pretty damn well." It was the right speech at the right time and gave the team confidence for the rest of the year. The Bruins won at Penn State the next game, before beating Syracuse at home and earning a tough tie against Missouri on the road. Then the young Bruins went on a roll and collected five straight wins.

The fifth victory came at the expense of crosstown rival USC. The Bruins won 20–16 and clinched the conference title and a trip to the Rose Bowl—and a rematch with Michigan State on New Year's Day. Before that, though, was a trip to Prothro's hometown of Knoxville and a game against the Tennessee Volunteers.

In the beginning, it wasn't pretty. Both teams had come from nowhere during the year. The Bruins were headed to the Rose Bowl, and the Volunteers were going to the Bluebonnet Bowl. This was in an era when either you won your league, or you waited until next year. There were not a couple dozen bowl games like today, when a team can play .500 ball and get to a bowl. This Tennessee team played tough and stingy defense—they had allowed only 14 points all year! So when the Volunteers jumped on UCLA for 3 touchdowns in the first half, things looked pretty bleak for the Bruins. Tennessee took a 21–0 lead into the locker room for the halftime break.

Head coach Tommy Prothro is carried off the field after UCLA won the Rose Bowl on January 1, 1966. AP/Wide World

"You have embarrassed me in front of my hometown!" Prothro shouted at his team. He turned around and walked out. That was it. Short, and not so sweet—but definitely to the point.

What followed was a wild second half that made this Bruins team know it could accomplish greatness. There are people in Tennessee who still talk about the game as one of the best ever. UCLA lost 37–34, but what a comeback!

It was at that point and no other—even during the five-game winning streak—that Beban and his teammates realized, "Hey we're pretty good!" They were young, but what a schedule they played in 1965 for their new head coach. Plus, now they would get a season-ending rematch with Michigan State, the team that pinned their ears back in the opening game of the year.

On New Year's Day 1966, more than 100,000 fans jammed the Rose Bowl in Pasadena. The Bruins were ranked fifth in the nation, and they were playing the number-one team, Michigan State.

The Spartans were undefeated at 10–0 and were feeling good about the rematch. They had already beaten UCLA once that year—why not again? The Bruins took the lead in the second quarter on Beban's 1-yard run. Beban ran 1 yard for another score, and UCLA led 14–0 at halftime. The second score was set up by a daring onside kick recovered by UCLA's Dallas Grider. Farr had a beautiful run of 21 yards, then Beban connected with Altenberg for a 20-yard gain to the 1 yard line.

But Michigan State came back. After scoring twice, they tried for a two-point conversion both times and failed. Defensive back Bob Stiles made a game-saving tackle on the second try, and UCLA won 14–12. It was the Bruins, first Rose Bowl victory.

The Bruins started 1966 with a seven-game winning streak and went 9–1. In 1967 they were 7–2–1. Beban amassed more than 1,500 yards total offense and scored 11 touchdowns. When the Heisman votes were counted, he had edged out USC tailback O. J. Simpson to win the award in one of the closest races ever.

Beban finished his career with 35 touchdown runs and still ranks fourth on UCLA's all-time list. He is eighth in passing (with 4,087 yards) and fifth in total offense (5,358 yards). A member of the UCLA Hall of Fame, he was a second-round pick of the NFL's Los Angeles Rams in 1968 and eventually played two years for the Washington Redskins, including one under legendary coach Vince Lombardi.

What a ride it was for Gary Beban. Bruins fans are glad the man from the north decided to come south.

The Man for Twenty Seasons

Twenty years as the head coach of the UCLA football team is a long time. It means a lot of film and video broken down preparing for the next game or the next season. It means constantly evaluating personnel. It's the nonstop job of a head football coach. Terry Donahue held the position in Westwood from 1976 to 1995. During that time he became the winningest coach in the history of the Pac-10 conference. Time consuming? Yes. Rewarding? Absolutely. Donahue calls his stint coaching at UCLA "the most exciting years of my life."

Donahue grew up in Sherman Oaks, California, and went to Notre Dame High School there. After Donahue finished his prep years as a linebacker, he played freshman football at San Jose State. When that didn't quite work out like he thought, he returned home to Southern California and attended L. A. Valley College, then enrolled at UCLA. He didn't know it at the time, but that transfer would change his life forever.

Never in his wildest imagination did he think that someday he would be the head coach at the Westwood campus. When he first got to UCLA, he just wanted to make the Bruin team and play football—the thought of coaching never even entered his mind.

Donahue was a walk-on for head coach Tommy Prothro in 1964. Everybody knows what people think of walk-ons—long shot! "That guy has about as much chance to make this team as a snowball on Wilshire Boulevard in July," according to one player. But Donahue not only loved the challenge, he relished it. What an opportunity—to play football at one of the greatest universities in the world. Could he do it? Oh, yes, he could. Taking that challenge would be the beginning of Terry Donahue's legacy at UCLA.

Terry redshirted the 1964 season, then he earned a shot at playing time in 1965. He battled his way into a starting spot at defensive tackle that he would hold for the next two years. Donahue was listed at 6' 1" and never over 200 pounds—small for the defensive line, even then, but a great example of the "gutty little Bruin." Don-

Terry Donahue was head coach of UCLA during the golden age from 1976 to 1995.
AP/Wide World

ahue wasn't huge, but he was gutty. Over the next two seasons, Terry started every game as UCLA won seventeen of twenty-one games, including an upset of Michigan State in the 1966 Rose Bowl.

It was while playing for Prothro that Donahue started to think about the future and about coaching. Prothro had been an assistant on the great Red Sanders teams of the 1950s. He was a winner, a fierce competitor, and a field general on game day. Preparation was his forte. Donahue took notice. He studied and learned while playing, and it paid off. After graduation, he decided that his future was in coaching.

Donahue built his coaching foundation the hard way—with good, old-fashioned hard work. His first stop was at the University of Kansas with former UCLA assistant Pepper Rodgers. At the age of twenty-three, Donahue became one of the youngest assistants in the country on the Division I level.

Donahue was in charge of the defensive line for the Jay-hawks, and he coached the way he played. "Okay, men. Let's get down, and let's get dirty," he'd say—meaning, don't be afraid to get some grass stains and grime on your uniform. The players looked up to him. This coach played their position and started at UCLA. He played in the Rose Bowl. If he talked about how to fight off a block or rush the passer, they listened.

Terry coached four years at Kansas, picking up valuable experience along the way. His first big break came in 1971, when Rodgers left Kansas and took Donahue along for the ride. And what a ride it would be for Donahue, leading him back to Southern California where Rodgers was the new head coach at UCLA.

At UCLA Donahue initially was in charge of the offensive line. The change would benefit him for the rest of his coaching days, especially when he became a head coach. How many times have you heard football people talk about the game being won or lost on the offensive and defensive lines? It really is true.

Donahue handled the offensive line for the next five seasons, three under Rodgers and then two more years for Dick Vermeil (1974 and 1975). The experience helped round out his solid foundation as an all-around football coach—he knew both sides of the football equally as well.

After Vermeil put together two solid years at UCLA—the 1975 team finished 9–2–1 and topped it off with a huge win in the Rose Bowl over number-one Ohio State 23–10—he headed for the NFL where he was named the new head coach of the Philadelphia Eagles.

Now came Terry Donahue's big opportunity. Tom Landry, the legendary coach of the Dallas Cowboys, used to say people were fortunate "when preparation meets opportunity." Donahue was prepared. And in February of 1976, he got his opportunity.

Terry was a thirty-one-year-old, good-looking guy who reminded folks of someone who lived next door on a primetime television show. The UCLA administration liked what they saw, too: a solid man with good credentials. Donahue was named the Bruins new head football coach.

Terry had plenty of experience, and he was ready. True, he was young—but this young man already had a maturity beyond his years. His youth gave him an energy that he never lost during his twenty years as head coach. Even up to that final year in West-wood in 1995, no coach ran a practice with more enthusiasm and vigor than Donahue. To watch him was amazing. He acted like a rookie coach every day—not in knowledge, of course, but in his

Pep Talk

Quarterback Tom Ramsey tells the story of coach Donahue getting into it with then-Wolverines head coach Bo Schembechler when the teams played early in 1982 at Michigan. As both teams went into the locker room at halftime, "Terry was hot about some of the tactics of the Michigan players during the game," says Ramsey. "He yelled at Schembechler running off the field at the half, 'So you're number one, eh?' and the Wolverine coach yelled back. I have never, ever, seen Donahue as livid and as focused at the same time between halves. He was so intense and fired up that it inspired the whole team. We went out and kicked some major butt in the second half and won 31–27."

Later that season, UCLA beat the Wolverines again, winning 24–14 in the Rose Bowl on New Year's Day.

constant excitement at practice. His energy was unreal. But that was Terry. If he did something, he did it all the way.

In 1976, in Donahue's first game as the UCLA coach, the Bruins upset favored Arizona State by a score of 28–10. Terry went on to lead the Bruins to a 9–2–1 record that year. But that was just the beginning.

In the beginning Donahue's teams transitioned from the Wishbone-Veer offense to what Terry called, "a balanced wide-open attack," and some critics didn't believe it could be pulled off. Donahue never wanted to abandon the running game. He had great running backs teamed with solid quarterbacks who could throw the ball to quick receivers. Right up until his retirement, UCLA's offense was built that way. Being a former defensive player, he recruited some of the tops in the country to play on the other side of the ball, too.

Donahue knew way back as a player the importance of the USC–UCLA game. USC was the pinnacle of college football in the 1970s—the standard everyone was shooting for. As a coach, he learned quickly that he had to win that game—maybe not every year, but enough times—or he wasn't going to keep his job. Donahue and his staff placed an importance on the L. A. championship right from the beginning, and it paid off. UCLA would go on to win eight straight against the Trojans in the 1990s. Donahue got his first win over USC in 1980, when running back Freeman McNeil caught a long touchdown pass from quarterback Jay Schroeder with just two minutes left to give UCLA a 20–17 victory. "I started out 0–4 against them," Donahue says. "We had to get that turned around, and we did. At the end of it we were 10–9–1 against those guys." Donahue closed out his career with five straight wins over the Trojans, the first five of the Bruins record eight straight victories in the series.

Being a head coach at the collegiate level is more than just practice during the week and running the team on Saturdays. The coach also is part of the academic community, concerned with players' grades and achievements. Constant recruiting and speaking engagements are part of the job, too. So having the right staff to help on the field is significant. As a coach one of the best things Donahue did was evaluate talent. He could spot talent in an athlete, and he could spot talent in assistant coaches, too— over a twenty-year period, he found plenty.

Two-Decade Man

Here's Terry Donahue's year-by-year record in his twenty seasons as coach of the Bruins:

Year	Record	Bowl
1976	9–2–1	Liberty
1977	7–4–0	
1978	8–3–1	Fiesta
1979	5–6–0	
1980	9–2–0	
1981	7–4–1	Bluebonnet
1982	10–1–1	Rose
1983	7–4–1	Rose
1984	9–3–0	Fiesta
1985	9–2–1	Rose
1986	8–3–1	Freedom
1987	10–2–0	Aloha
1988	10–2–0	Cotton
1989	3–7–1	
1990	5–6–0	
1991	9–3–0	Hancock
1992	6–5–0	
1993	8–4–0	Rose
1994	5–6–0	
1995	7–5–0	Aloha
Totals	**151–74–8**	

One of the criticisms of Donahue was that he was too conservative. Donahue took that one to heart in the late 1970s and into the 1980s. "I was a coach who was brought up with the running game," he says. "Many thought if we were going to compete with USC, we would have to throw the ball and have a sophisticated passing game. We needed to go out and talk about excitement and entertainment and attract some of the best athletes to help us win at this level, and that's what we did." Even though the conservative label stuck, Terry had some of college football's most prolific passers in the 1980s and 1990s.

Going to UCLA as a player and then becoming the head coach meant a lot to the former San Fernando Valley kid. The tradition, folklore, and history of the school were special to him. He always tried to remember the past and build on it. "I never tried to separate myself from the Red Sanders, Tommy Prothro, Pepper Rodgers, or Dick Vermeil eras," he says. "It was critical to teach the players in the program how much the past meant. Former players and coaches had contributed energy, effort, and hard work to establish our tradition. I had a real appreciation and respect for that."

Donahue is proud of his legacy at UCLA, and he is the first to acknowledge that it would not have happened without the help of many good people. "No one does it alone. I had plenty of help." Terry is humble. He was the central figure in building a good program over a long period of time, and he had as good a run as any coach can have in college football.

Of Quarterbacks and Roses

The 1980s would be noteworthy for the start of a special streak for head coach Terry Donahue and his UCLA Bruins. After dropping the 1981 Bluebonnet Bowl 33–14 to Michigan, UCLA began a string of eight consecutive bowl wins with a 24–14 victory over the Wolverines in the Rose Bowl on New Year's Day, 1983. And to make it even sweeter, the bowl streak was forged entirely against quality football programs—

Arkansas, Brigham Young, Florida, Illinois (twice), Iowa, Miami, and Michigan were the name schools that fell to the Bruins.

When a school wins big like the young men from Westwood did during the 1980s, it undoubtedly has good players at every position. Some of the UCLA players from that decade have become household names to Bruins fans, and many went on to play in the NFL.

There are several memorable victories in UCLA's impressive bowl-winning streak, but one that really stands out was the Bruins 45–28 victory over Iowa in the 1986 Rose Bowl. The win was memorable not only because UCLA upset a favored Hawkeye team that was ranked fourth in nation but also because of the long road the Bruins traveled to get there.

The 1985 season began with a quarterback controversy. Senior David Norrie and junior Matt Stevens were battling to see who would be the number-one signal caller for UCLA. The vote was close, but the senior Norrie edged out the junior Stevens at the beginning of the season. Although Stevens wasn't jumping for joy about being second string, he buckled up his chin strap and went back to work.

The first game of the Bruins 1985 season was a big one at Brigham Young University. It was important not only because it was the first game of the year, but also because the Cougars were the defending national champs and entered the new season ranked eighth in the country. The Cougars were led by quarterback Robbie Bosco, a Heisman Trophy candidate.

Norrie, unaccustomed to being the starter, had first-game jitters and got off to a rough start. By the third quarter, Stevens replaced him at quarterback and helped the Bruins charge back

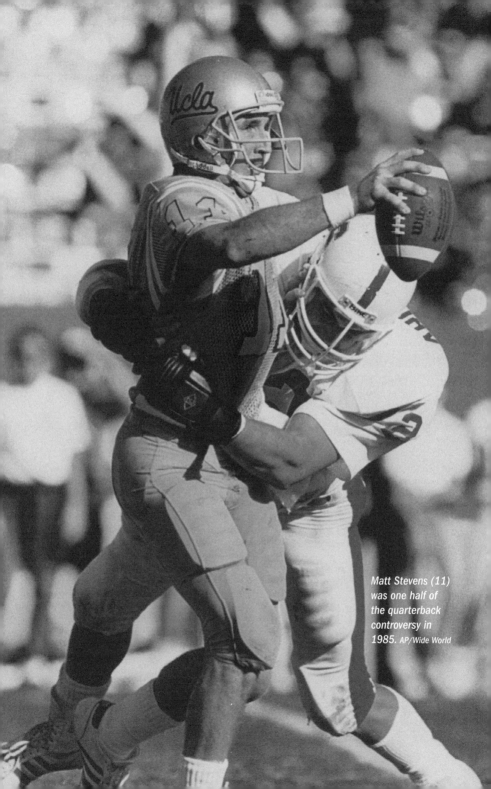

Matt Stevens (11) was one half of the quarterback controversy in 1985. AP/Wide World

Eight Is Enough

Here's UCLA's eight-game bowl winning streak under head coach Terry Donahue:

January 1, 1983	Rose Bowl	UCLA 24, Michigan 14
January 2, 1984	Rose Bowl	UCLA 45, Illinois 9
January 1, 1985	Fiesta Bowl	UCLA 39, Miami 37
January 1, 1986	Rose Bowl	UCLA 45, Iowa 28
December 30, 1986	Freedom Bowl	UCLA 31, BYU 10
December 25, 1987	Aloha Bowl	UCLA 20, Florida 16
January 2, 1989	Cotton Bowl	UCLA 17, Arkansas 3
December 31, 1991	Hancock Bowl	UCLA 6, Illinois 3

(The streak ended with Wisconsin's 21–16 victory over the Bruins on January 1, 1994.)

to win 27–24. Defensive back Craig Rutledge also made a huge play by intercepting a pass and returning it for a touchdown.

The quarterback controversy of 1985 continued, with Stevens number one going into the second game of the year at Tennessee against the Volunteers. But with the Bruins trailing at the half, the switch was on again. Norrie entered the game in the second half and led the way to one of the great comebacks of the 1980s.

UCLA was down by 16 points at 26–10 with 11:57 left to play when Norrie directed a 97-yard touchdown drive, capping the march with an 8-yard scoring toss to senior flanker Al Wilson. The big play of the drive was the quarterback's 44-yard pass to Mike Sherrard on third-and-10 from UCLA's 3 yard line. Norrie then hit a clutch two-point conversion, hooking up with tight end Jeff Ninowski—it was the senior's first catch. Now UCLA trailed by 8 points with 4:57 left. The Bruins defense stopped Tennessee, and the Volunteers had to punt. UCLA got the ball back with 1:43 remaining.

Norrie went to work again. This time, a 73-yard drive ended with a touchdown pass to young Willie "Flipper" Anderson with just 37 seconds left on the clock. Then, in a gutsy move, a running play by Gaston Green was good for the two-point conversion to tie the score at 26–26.

The game ended that way. The Bruins had been staring at a loss. And while the tie wasn't a victory by any means, it did not go into the "L" column.

UCLA hosted San Diego State a week later, and the quarterback controversy was on again. It was a game in which even the third quarterback on the depth chart, Brendan McCracken, saw action. The Bruins won easily, 34–16. For the moment Norrie was back on top as the number-one quarterback, with a huge conference game next in Seattle against Washington.

The Huskies, who are always tough at home, went right after the Bruins. By the third quarter, with Norrie struggling, Donahue sent Stevens into the game. Donahue was tired of waiting for Norrie to come around and told Stevens that no matter what, he would finish the game. But on the quarterback's second play, Stevens got caught in a pileup and twisted his knee so badly that he had to be carried off the field. Norrie went back in the game and finished up at quarterback, but the Bruins lost 21–14 and fell to 2–1–1 to start the year.

The quarterback controversy was tough on everybody. UCLA had a hard-hitting defense led by linebackers Ken Norton Jr. and Carnell Lake, defensive end Mark Walen, and defensive backs James Washington, Craig Rutledge, and Darryl Henley. The running game was there and the wide receivers were good, so it was up to someone to get the job done consistently at quarterback.

This team knew it could go somewhere if it could get some good quarterback play. That's when the bell was answered, and Norrie found himself taking on the challenge and starting to put up the numbers. As the season went on, his completion percentage was one of the highest in the nation. He would finish 1985 with a completion rate of 63.6 percent—the best in Bruins history at the time (and second now to another pretty good quarterback, Troy Aikman). Norrie helped UCLA run up six straight wins while putting up a lot of points on the board. The winning streak included a 1-point thriller in the Pallouse against the Washington State Cougars (31–30). The Bruins began thinking about the Rose Bowl. They could clinch a berth in the game by beating USC in their last game of the regular season.

UCLA wanted the Rose Bowl badly, and they wanted a win over USC even more. They could win the league outright if they beat the Trojans. In fact many of the players said they didn't care about the January 1 game if they couldn't beat their crosstown rival.

But a win wasn't in the cards for the Bruins that day. The team lost at the Coliseum, 17–13. To say UCLA's players were down in the dumps after the game is putting it mildly. Some of these guys were downright inconsolable. Jim McCullough, the big offensive tackle for UCLA, was so hot after the loss that he actually walked back to Westwood from South Central Los Angeles. His dad followed slowly behind him in a car to make sure he made it back. McCullough was still burning when he got back to the Westside. It summed up the mood of most of the ball club.

Now the Bruins would have to wait the rest of the afternoon for the outcome of the Arizona–Arizona State game. The Wildcats would have to win for the Bruins to win the league and get to the Rose Bowl. Arizona did get by the Sun Devils, and UCLA would represent the Pac-10 on New Year's Day in Pasadena.

Coach Donahue got the team together the following day to make the announcement official. Even though many of the players were still stinging from the loss to USC, they started to get excited about playing the University of Iowa. Head coach Hayden Fry's Hawkeyes were ranked number four in the country. The Bruins had been in the top ten until losing to USC and dropping to fourteenth.

Iowa had lost only once. The challenge was there. By the end of the day, players were not only excited but also ready to redeem themselves from the loss to USC—or to at least try to forget it and move on. They were going to the Rose Bowl, and they were the Pac-10 conference champs.

Iowa was led by quarterback Chuck Long and running back Ronnie Harmon on offense. On defense the Hawkeyes featured linebacker Larry Station and the toughest unit in the Big Ten. This defense was predicated on lining up the same way for every single down. They would then fall into a two-deep, five-under or a three-deep, four-under in their pass coverage. Then, depending on which formation they went into, the defensive line would slant to try to confuse the offensive team. Coach Fry had formulated this so opponents would be baffled most of the time. It was really a roll of the dice for the offense to figure out which defense Iowa would be in on any given play.

The Bruins had a month to prepare for the big game in the Arroyo Seco, and they spent that time learning as much as they could about the Iowa powerhouse. In the final week before the showdown, Norrie pulled a hamstring muscle in his leg. After playing so well down the stretch of the season, he would have to sit out the big bowl game.

This is where the genius of Coach Donahue paid dividends. With Norrie out, Stevens was the man—again. Because of the high level of competition between Norris and Stevens during the year, there was no lack of confidence among the Bruins with Stevens back as the starting quarterback. Stevens had been a starter, and he had the experience. He was the man the Bruins would have to count on to knock off the Hawkeyes. And for the week before the January 1 game, he took all the reps in practice, studied, and reviewed film. He was ready.

Three days before the game, UCLA offensive coordinator Homer Smith picked up a valuable tip from watching tape on Iowa. He noticed that the nose guard was giving away what defense was going to be run. If the nose guard's feet were parallel, the line would slant to the left. If his feet were staggered, they would slant to the right. By knowing which way the line was attacking, he also could figure out the defensive coverage of the secondary. Homer had found a way to solve the defense that had fooled the Big Ten all year! All of a sudden, there was no mystery. The Bruins would use this to their advantage.

Kicking Is for the Kickers

When quarterback David Norrie pulled his hamstring leading up to the 1986 Rose Bowl, he did it while kicking footballs at practice the week before the game. As a result of his injury, he didn't play in UCLA's 45–28 victory over Iowa.

If the Iowa nose guard was tipping left, the UCLA signal called at the line would be Los Angeles or Portland, signifying the left side of the United States. If the defense was giving away the fact that they were going right, the signal would be Boston or New York, the right side of the country. It was ingenious. Iowa never knew what hit them.

More than 103,000 fans packed the stadium on New Year's Day. The players woke up on game day from a restless sleep. At 9:00 A.M. they ate a breakfast of eggs, bacon, hash browns, spaghetti, and juice or milk, and then they were off to the Rose Bowl by 10:30 A.M. The game was scheduled for 2:00 P.M. They had to get taped, stretch, and loosen up, and they wanted to be there early.

The quarterbacks and receivers were the first ones on the field for warm-ups. Stevens recalls standing in the tunnel, waiting to go on the field. The players said they could feel the electricity in the air all the way through their bones. As Stevens stuck his head out from underneath the stadium, the Bruins fans erupted. Stevens wasn't supposed to go out on the field yet, but the magnetism pulled him in and he raced across the natural grass to the bench. "I never felt my feet hit the ground," he says.

The Bruins were confident. They had studied their individual keys all week. To a man, they felt well coached. Though they were surprised by the size of Iowa's players—this Hawkeye team was huge—the Bruins soon discovered that they were quicker and faster than Iowa, and they exploited those differences the entire game. UCLA, especially on the offensive line, got off the ball quicker than its opponent. Mike Hartmeier, Jim McCullough, Duval Love, Bob Cox, and Joe Goebel were the big men up front who protected the quarterback and opened up holes all day.

Green pulled a hamstring early in the game, but the Bruins never skipped a beat. Ball, a 6'2", 225-pound redshirt freshman running back from Ypsilanti, Michigan, entered the game and dominated. He made a name for himself by rushing for 227 yards and 4 touchdowns. Stevens mixed in the passing game by completing sixteen of twenty-six attempts for 189 yards and a touchdown to Sherrard. The quarterback also had a 1-yard run for a touchdown when Ball said he was exhausted. The Bruins rolled to victory.

Even though Long passed for 319 yards, the Bruins limited the Hawkeyes to just 82 yards rushing and limited their star running back, Harmon, to just 55 yards and no touchdowns. In fact Harmon had trouble holding on to the ball and fumbled four times.

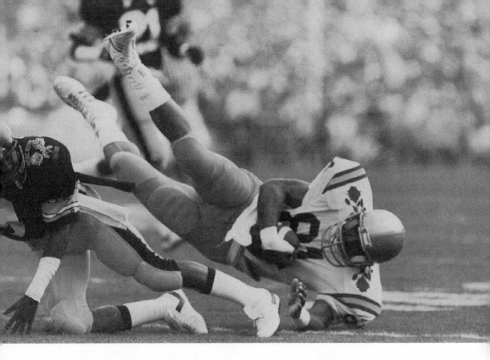

Tight end Derek Tennell pulls in a pass for a first down against Iowa in the Rose Bowl on January 1, 1986. AP/Wide World

The Bruins were Rose Bowl champions for the third time in four seasons. They also ended their season with a bowl victory for the fourth consecutive year. That string would reach seven when Donahue led his teams to bowl wins each year through 1988. The eighth and final win in the bowl streak came in 1991.

Three-Time All-American

Everybody loves to see scoring in sports. The three-run home run in baseball, the slam dunk or a big three-pointer in basketball, and the long touchdown pass or run in football are exciting. But all successful coaches talk about defense. Teams win with defense. More often than not, championship teams play solid, if not outstanding, defense. It really doesn't matter what sport it is, defense wins.

Let's face it. If you score 100 points in a basketball game but give up 101, you lose. Hold that team to 99, and you win. On a baseball team, they talk about being strong up the middle.

In football a team needs defensive players who want to hit, fight off blocks, play good pass defense, rush the passer, and just flat out have a desire to tackle. Red Sanders, the legendary UCLA football coach, simply figured that the team that blocks and tackles the best wins the game. His theory was that by blocking better than the opponent, a team gives its passer, running back, and punter time to execute. A team that tackles better than the opposition will stop its enemy on the other side of the line of scrimmage and get the ball back.

The Bruins have had more than their share of standouts on the defensive side of the ball. Perhaps the greatest impact came from linebacker Jerry Robinson, who arguably is the best defensive player to date in UCLA history. The numbers back it up. Robinson is the Bruins all-time career leader with 468 tackles. He was the first consensus three-time All-American at UCLA (1976 to 1978) and the first college player to be so honored since SMU's legendary Doak Walker (1947 to 1949).

Robinson was considered for the Heisman Trophy as college football's most outstanding player in 1978. He finished tenth, which was unheard of at the time for a defensive player. He's in both the UCLA Hall of Fame and the National Football Foundation College Hall of Fame. What is even more astounding is that Robinson was recruited to play wide receiver at UCLA.

Robinson's athletic career began when he played soccer as a youngster at Cook Junior High School in Santa Rosa, California. "I was a soccer player first," Robinson says. "It was only when the two seasons crossed over, that I was introduced to football."

In the beginning Robinson didn't want to play football. He wanted to play baseball and soccer. But when he started playing Pop Warner, he got the football bug. In his first year of organized football, his team won a championship while he was playing defensive end. And that was it—he was hooked. Goodbye, soccer—hello, football.

Like so many great athletes, Robinson played different sports in high school: football, basketball, and baseball. In fact he says one reason he eventually chose to attend UCLA was because of John Wooden and his teachings about basketball and about life. As a senior at Cardinal Newman High School, Robinson was a third-team All-American center in basketball. Secretly, he hoped he could play both sports when he went to Westwood, even though that never happened.

As the years passed in high school, baseball moved too slow for Robinson. In football, he started out as a running back, but was bored. When he moved to defense, his senses came alive at nose guard. That's right, Robinson played on the defensive line and also played tight end as a prep.

Robinson knew coming out of high school that he was going to UCLA. Santa Rosa is not exactly around the corner from Westwood, but it was close enough to home that he could see his mother when he wanted. Funny thing, though. As Robinson puts it, "I figured that if I went to UCLA and football didn't work out, I could play basketball for John Wooden. The only problem was, when I got there Coach Wooden retired." Football was going to be Jerry Robinson's sport all the way—he just didn't know it then.

Robinson lettered as a wideout his freshman year at UCLA. He and teammate Manu Tuiasosopo, who was a defensive lineman, were the only freshmen who were on the Bruins travel squad in 1975. At that time, it never entered his mind that the following year he would be an All-American—and make it as a linebacker!

In 1975 defensive coordinator Lynn Stiles would ask the young wide receiver after every game, "How many balls did you catch and how many plays were you involved with in the game today?" Robinson didn't quite catch on until the end of his freshman year, when Stiles and head coach Dick Vermeil talked with him after the USC game about preparing to play linebacker when the Bruins went to the Rose Bowl to face Ohio State on New Year's Day. They told him that with his speed and agility, he could revolutionize the position. They felt he could get ready in time for the big game, which was still a month away. Robinson agreed to consider the move, though he had no idea what lay ahead.

Robinson's teammates knew of the meeting in the coach's office. "What's up?" they asked. When Robinson told them he might be moving to linebacker, they were shocked. "Oh, brother, you are going to get killed," they said. "You're a wide receiver. Are you crazy? They'll eat you alive!"

When Robinson heard that from his teammates, he thought, "That's it. I'm going to do it. I'm going to make the move to linebacker. These guys don't really know me and don't know what's in my heart and how competitive I really am." His teammates didn't know it, but they had just stoked a fire in Robinson that would burn for years to come.

Robinson had something to prove. He was 6' 3" and weighed 208 pounds. He was light for the position of inside linebacker even then, but he was very quick. One intangible that his pals didn't figure into the equation was that he loved contact. He liked to hit. With all of those components working together, he was ready to

Jerry Robinson (84) was perhaps the greatest defensive player in UCLA history.
College Football Hall of Fame

become one of the best collegiate linebackers in the country.

Robinson loved the challenge. He knew that an offensive player knows where he is going and how fast he will get there. Most of the time, a linebacker's first move is back and read, then react. The advantage is to the ball carrier or receiver and to the offensive lineman trying to block a linebacker to open up holes to move the ball downfield. For Robinson, that was the real challenge.

"I never thought about making All-American," Robinson says. "That's not why I played the position. I played because I enjoyed playing the game. It's competitive, and I'm a competitive guy. For somebody to tell me I couldn't do it because I was too small was more of an incentive. It motivated me to be the best that I could possibly be."

And, man, he was one of the best. Robinson combined with players such as Tuiasosopo and Easley to give the Bruins a stifling defense in the late 1970s. "With Tuiasosopo at nose guard, Robinson at linebacker, and Easley at safety," former offensive coordinator Bob Field says, "an offense that wanted to go up the middle was in trouble."

The fire burned inside Robinson for a long time—three more years in college and then thirteen in the NFL with the Philadelphia Eagles and Los Angeles Raiders. He made believers out of everyone who told him he couldn't make the move to defense.

When Robinson first came to UCLA, he wore number 84. After he switched to linebacker, he kept the number. He is so proud of the fact that teams used to look at him, especially in the beginning, and say, "Look, they have a wide receiver playing linebacker." He knew what they were thinking, and it made him even more determined. They were in for a surprise.

Career Achievement

Here are a few of UCLA linebacker Jerry Robinson's statistical highlights:

INTERCEPTIONS RETURNED FOR TOUCHDOWNS
95 yards vs. Minnesota (1977)
72 yards vs. Washington State (1976)
69 yards vs. Stanford (1976)

TACKLES IN A GAME
28 vs. Air Force (1976)
23 vs. USC (1977)
21 vs. Kansas (1977)
21 vs. USC (1978)
20 vs. Minnesota (1978)
18 vs. Oregon (1978), Stanford (1977), USC (1976),
   Ohio State (1976), Arizona (1976)

On New Year's Day 1976, Ohio State was one team that couldn't believe that number 84 was warming up at linebacker. This was the same young freshman who had caught a couple of passes earlier in the year when these teams met in the Coliseum (UCLA lost that game to the Buckeyes 41–20, but the Bruins would topple the nation's top-ranked team in the Rose Bowl 23–10). In fact Robinson's first play was a tackle on running back Archie Griffin, a two-time winner of the Heisman Trophy, sweeping around end. Can you imagine what Woody Hayes'

"Dee-fense, Dee-Fense"

There have been some great All-Americans at UCLA who played defense. And there are some who never got such national recognition but who, nevertheless, were excellent. The old-timers had to go both ways on offense and defense. But just because you were good at halfback didn't mean you were a standout on defense in the old days. Sometimes a coach had to take that into consideration in the days before the platoon system took over. Not everybody could be like Bob Waterfield, who was not only a great passer and runner, he also had 7 interceptions on defense one year. Here are some Bruins (in addition to Jerry Robinson) who deserve recognition for their play on the defensive side of the ball:

■ Linebacker Donn Moomaw was UCLA's first bona fide two-time All-American, when he earned the honors in 1950 and 1952. It wasn't until 1966 that another Bruins defender was named an All-American. Defensive lineman John Richardson made it from a UCLA club that finished fifth in the Associated Press rankings that year. He weighed 256 pounds, which was huge for that era.

■ Don Manning played in that same era and was an All-American linebacker in 1967. He and quarterback Gary Beban were the first Bruins to become consensus All-Americans. In the three years they played together (1965 to 1967), UCLA's overall record was 24–5–2.

■ In 1973 Jimmy Allen became the first of many Bruins defensive backs to earn All-American status. Oscar Edwards was selected in 1976 and the hard-hitting Kenny Easley in 1978, his first of three years in a row. "Nobody was more of a punishing hitter

Linebacker Donn Moomaw with coach Red Sanders in 1952. AP/Wide World

than Easley," says former UCLA assistant coach Bob Field. "He practiced hard and set the bar high for the other players by never taking a day off." Easley was the Bruins second three-time All-American, after Jerry Robinson.

- Another superb defensive back was Don Rodgers, an All-American safety in 1983.

- In 1988 Darryl Henley was a consensus selection at corner-back. Safeties Eric Turner (1990) and Matt Darby (1991) also earned All-American honors. Safeties Marvin Goodwin (as a junior in 1993) and Shaun Williams (as a senior in 1997) were the most-recent UCLA defensive backs to be recognized as All-Americans.

- In 2001, linebacker Robert Thomas earned All-American status. Two years later, Dave Ball, a great defensive end, was another consensus selection.

- Jamir Miller, an All-American in 1993, could dominate a game at linebacker. Several other excellent UCLA linebackers have been named All-Americans, too, including Roman Phifer in 1990, Carnell Lake in 1988 (he would become a tremendous defensive back in the NFL), and Ken Norton, Jr. in 1987.

- Two defensive linemen from the 1970s were All-Americans: end Fred McNeill in 1973 and nose guard Cliff Frazier in 1975. McNeill went on to play linebacker in the NFL for 13 years with the Minnesota Vikings.

coaching staff was thinking? "Hey, this skinny wide receiver just brought down our star running back."

That was just the beginning for Robinson. "The offensive lineman were looking at me wearing my number 84, thinking that I'm still a wide receiver, and they were going to have me for lunch," Robinson says. "I thought, 'Well, no you're not.'"

Robinson says he was blessed with good coaching from the beginning. Way back in high school it was Ed Lloyd, who ran Cardinal Newman's program when Robinson was getting his feet wet in football as a prep. Lloyd stressed the fundamentals. "His techniques were my foundation for success, even though I didn't realize it at the time," says Robinson. In college Robinson was fortunate enough not only to play for Vermeil and Stiles, but also UCLA assistant Jed Hughes, who was fanatical about his players working hard and being in better shape than their opponents. These coaches all had one thing in common: They all stressed the fundamentals and techniques of sure tackling, taking on blockers, and, most importantly, stepping with the correct foot.

"It was the little things that made the difference," Robinson says. When the Bruins would look at video, the coaches might say, "Do you know why you missed this tackle? Your head is on the wrong side."

"It sounds simple, but you had to have your head in the proper position—in front of the ball carrier, not behind him," Robinson says. "If you have your head in front, across the bow [as in the front of a boat], and wrap your arms, you'll bring him down. That is as simple as it gets."

Simple, yes, but it takes talent, too, and Jerry Robinson had plenty of that.

The King of Texas

It's January 1998. The Bruins are in the middle of a twenty-game winning streak and are in Dallas to play Texas A&M in the Cotton Bowl. It's halftime, and UCLA is losing to the Aggies 16–7. As halftime unfolds, the bands are playing, the show's beginning, and country stars from the Nashville Network are ready to perform. Up in the press box, it's time to eat. But hold everything. All eyes are on the back of the room, where someone has just entered. It's Dallas Cowboys quarterback and UCLA alum Troy Aikman—Mr. Super Bowl himself—here to see his old team and meet the newest quarterback sensation at UCLA, Cade McNown.

Everyone watches as Aikman pours two large scoops of chili into a bowl, adds onions and a little cheese, and sits down to eat. Everyone watches! They watch him eat every bite, as if he is a king. But we *are* in Texas, and in Texas this great athlete is king. He really is. Dallas loves winners, and Aikman is definitely a winner—he has three Super Bowl rings to prove it.

As a youngster growing up in Cerritos, California, Aikman played football, basketball, and baseball. In fact in Frontier Little League in Cerritos, Aikman played with several pals who would later become pro baseball players. Although baseball was his true passion, the sport took a backseat to football when Aikman and his family moved to Henryetta, Oklahoma. In Henryetta you rooted for the Sooners of Oklahoma or the Cowboys of Oklahoma State, and the move to football country pushed twelve-year-old Troy toward the gridiron.

By the time Aikman graduated from Henryetta High School, Oklahoma, Oklahoma State, Missouri, Tennessee, and Arkansas, among other schools, were interested in the strong-armed young talent who looked like a fullback, linebacker, or tight end, and who could throw—and throw accurately.

At first Aikman committed to Oklahoma State (whose football coach was Jimmy Johnson, for whom Aikman would play in Dallas during his NFL career), but before he started he wanted

Troy Aikman played for two
stellar seasons at UCLA.
AP/Wide World

to take one more trip—to Norman to check out the Sooners. With the Sooners he was sold on the fact he would have the chance to win a national championship, to win the Big Eight title, and to play in the Orange Bowl. He became a Sooner. Although Aikman doubted whether he could quarterback in Division I football, he wanted to find out. After just two weeks on campus and a few practices, he realized that he could compete at quarterback on that level.

What's interesting about Aikman is that as a youngster he actually got burned out playing quarterback. He had been playing the position his entire young life. So when he moved from Southern California to Oklahoma, he told his new coach in the eighth grade that he wanted to play fullback. For two years, he played fullback. But like a lot of young kids, he changed his mind again. After running the ball for a while, he was ready to get back under center and play quarterback again. He had missed it. That was his calling.

"I was always the biggest kid on every team I played on," says Troy. "But by my freshman year, I was ready to go back to quarterback and lucky to have a freshman coach who let me do it. I never played any other position again." And the rest is history.

A lot of people wondered why a throwing quarterback would play at Oklahoma for a coach, Barry Switzer, who used the Wishbone offense. Well, during his last year in high school, as Aikman tells it, "Oklahoma had lost to USC during the regular season, and Switzer had Marcus Dupree as a running back. The coach decided to abandon the Wishbone and go to the I-formation and let Dupree do his thing." One problem, though:

Dupree left the program, later transferring to Mississippi State.

The Sooners told Aikman that they were going to stay in the I-formation offensively and that the Wishbone was old-fashioned and gone. But there were mixed signals. Aikman was also told in the recruiting process that the next year's starting quarterback, Danny Bradley, was an option quarterback. Oklahoma would run some of the option offense Bradley's senior year, but go strictly to the I-formation in Troy's sophomore year.

Keith Jackson, who would become an All-American tight end and was recruited in the same class with Aikman, was told the same thing. But others in Aikman's recruiting class were told the team was going back to the Wishbone. "Half the class thought we were going to Oklahoma with an I-back formation and throwing the football, and the other half was told, 'We are going back to the Wishbone and do what we have always done,'" says Aikman. After Aikman's freshman year, Switzer announced that he kind of liked the Wishbone, and he was going to stick with it.

It all came to a head the next season, when Aikman broke his leg in a game against Miami. Not only was he out for the rest of the year with the injury, he just didn't feel he fit in with the option offense. Jamelle Holieway stepped in at quarterback as a true freshman to run the offense, and he led the team to the Big Eight championship. He was the conference's offensive player of the year, and the Sooners won the national championship to boot. The handwriting was on the wall. Even though Switzer said there would be an open competition the next season, Aikman knew it was time to move on.

The coach knew Troy wanted to transfer. Instead of being angry, Switzer helped his young quarterback find a new home. "He understood and was very supportive," Aikman says. "He immediately got on the phone, pulled out a list of the top passing teams in the country, and started calling those head coaches for me." Switzer called Hayden Fry at Iowa, Lavelle Edwards at BYU, Jack Elway at Stanford, and Terry Donahue at UCLA.

Aikman had a plan. Since he didn't want to go head-to-head with an established starter, every school he was seriously considering during his redshirt season had a senior quarterback. Miami, where Jimmy Johnson had become the head coach, had senior quarterback Vinny Testaverde. Arizona State was another consideration, with Jeff Van Raaphorst as the Sun Devils senior signal caller. Iowa, which had Chuck Long in his last year at quarterback, was a contender, and so was UCLA, with senior Matt Stevens at the controls for the Bruins.

Aikman planned trips to all the schools he was considering. His first stop was UCLA. In February 1986 he left cold and icy Norman, Oklahoma—where it was 25 degrees—and landed at LAX in Los Angeles, where it was a crystal clear day and a beautiful 75 degrees. Oh, what a recruiting tool!

When Aikman arrived, Bill Rees, UCLA's recruiting coordinator, took him out to lunch at a restaurant on the water in Malibu. During lunch, Troy asked Rees, "How far is the school from here?" "Oh, it's about ten minutes," Rees replied. As Aikman puts it, "I pretty much knew at that moment I was going to be signing with UCLA." Aikman had lived in Cerritos as a youngster and liked the area. And he wasn't the first or last person

Practice Makes Perfect

When Aikman was at UCLA, the defense and offense would go eight-on-eight every day at practice. "Going against Aikman and crew for twenty-five plays daily made our defense that much better," says Bob Field, UCLA's defensive coordinator. "It really helped us win games. We weren't going to face a quarterback any better."

wooed by the beauty of the coast and the glorious weather in Southern California.

Matt Stevens's crew drew the assignment of hosting Aikman while he was visiting Westwood. Safety Craig Rutledge was there, too, and offensive lineman Jim McCullough. They all hit it off. In fact Stevens tells the story of a very pensive Jeff George, who would later go to the University of Illinois, being recruited at the same time. The consensus was, "Hey, we love this Aikman guy. We know he's good, he'll be super for the program, and he's really just one of the boys." They told the coaches that if it was a choice between the two, "Let's get Troy." And this was before anyone had seen either of the two even throw a ball. It turned out to be a great fit.

Before Aikman committed to the Bruins for his redshirt year, he talked with Coach Donahue. Troy didn't want to be a scout-team quarterback, and the Bruins coach had no problem with Aikman sitting out the season and working out, studying, looking at film, and really learning the offense. Assistant coach Rick Neuheisel, the former UCLA quarterback, became his personal tutor.

"There were some days we didn't even go out on the field," Troy says. "Rick would work with me and teach me about defenses and coverages and what the Bruins were doing within their offense. I learned a great deal about football at that time. So when my junior year came around, I was ready."

Of all the talents Aikman possessed, he admits that accuracy was one of his best. "I have always been able to put a football or baseball where I wanted it to go," he says. "Norv Turner [who coached with the Dallas Cowboys] said the same thing. I worked on it, but a lot of guys work on it. It was just something that had always been there since my younger days, and was one of my strengths as a quarterback."

Stevens tells the story about playing catch with Aikman for the first time. "I threw a ball to him, and then he threw a ball to me," Stevens says. "After catching his perfect spiral, with the perfect touch and accuracy, I said, 'Bring out the armor.'" He knew right then and there that the transfer from Oklahoma had it!

Donahue calls Aikman "the most accurate passer I've ever been around." The Bruins all-time record for completion percentage (minimum 200 completions) is proof of it: Aikman holds the mark at 64.8 percent. In his two seasons at UCLA

Troy Aikman gets nailed by Stanford's Chuck Robinson in a 1988 game. AP/Wide World

(1987 to 1988), he passed for 5,289 yards and 41 touchdowns.

Troy was the Pac-10's offensive player of the year in 1987, finished third in the balloting for the Heisman Trophy in 1988, and earned All-American honors both years. And even though he was part of the Bruins run of bowl victories in the 1980s (the Aloha Bowl to close the 1987 season and the Cotton Bowl to cap 1988), and his two years at UCLA produced 10–2 teams each season, he still feels that UCLA should have won a national championship with the players they had, but they came up short. "We were number one for a while my senior year, then lost to Washington State, and that knocked us out of the race," he says.

"I was part of a national championship team with Oklahoma and won three Super Bowl championships with the Cowboys," says Aikman. "My only regret was not getting UCLA to the Rose Bowl. Other than that, I feel like my career is complete."

Troy Aikman enjoyed playing for head coach Terry Donahue during his two seasons at UCLA. "Playing for Terry Donahue was special," he says. "We had a lot of characters and had a lot of fun with great chemistry—the head coach has to be applauded for that. First, just to be at UCLA meant you were smart. Donahue wanted players who were good people, too. And if they didn't do what they were supposed to, he wouldn't keep them around. I liked that."

Today, the relationships Aikman developed from his college and pro days are what he cherishes the most—some of his former teammates are his closest friends. "I'm proud of my years at

UCLA and I look back on them very fondly," says Aikman, who ended his NFL career following the 2000 season. "Some of my best years were spent on campus at UCLA."

The
Streak

It was a special time at UCLA, from early in the 1997 season until late in 1998. That's when the Bruins forged a school-record, twenty-game winning streak—the last ten games of 1997 and the first ten of the following year. UCLA's 1997 season began on August 30. For long-time football fans, that first game in late summer felt a little early. Nowadays, it's no big deal to start college football in August, but for some reason that trip to Washington State in Pullman seemed early. And it turned out to be a tough trip, too. The Cougars won, 37–34, and it felt particularly bad for the Bruins to lose.

UCLA had a chance to win this game. Skip Hicks, the Bruins great running back, had a terrific day. He rushed for 190 yards and 4 touchdowns. But with time running out in the game, backup Jermaine Lewis, a smaller back, was stopped on fourth-and-goal from the 1 yard line, just shy of a touchdown. UCLA thought Lewis had scored, but the officials spotted the ball an inch short of the goal line. Washington State's quarterback, Ryan Leaf, took over and ran out the final 2:48 to secure the win.

The Bruins had finished 1996 with a 5–6 mark, so this wasn't quite the start they wanted in 1997. But it didn't get any easier. They lost their home opener the following week to Tennessee, 30–24, after rallying to nearly topple the third-ranked Volunteers. Now UCLA was 0–2 to start the season. Nobody knew it then, but a school-record winning streak was about to captivate UCLA fans and football enthusiasts throughout the southland. The winning streak would start at, of all places, the University of Texas.

The University of Texas is in the city of Austin, and when Longhorns fans start talking football, they get *real* serious. It's not just limited to the city of Austin, either. Football is life itself in Texas, and the whole state loves the Longhorns. Oh, sure, you can talk about Texas A&M, SMU, Baylor, and the list goes on, but the one program that people get revved up about with a fervor is UT.

Texas entered the game with UCLA 1–0 and ranked number eleven in the country. Longhorn fans knew the Bruins were 0–2, and hopes were high for a big win. They were in for a letdown.

At UCLA, meanwhile, the coaches, fans, and administration were wondering what kind of a football team the Bruins were going to be. Cade McNown, a junior, was the quarterback. Hicks was one of the best running backs in the country. The Bruins had an excellent kicker in Chris Sailer. Mike Grieb was a terrific tight end. Not only could he catch the ball, but he also was like a sixth lineman up front, because of his blocking skills. McNown had one of his favorite targets, Jim "Mr. Breakaway" McElroy, to run pass routes. The lefty quarterback also knew that he was protected, because the men up front could block. And maybe, just maybe, when Cade was flushed out of the pocket, the tough little redhead could pick up some valuable yardage running the football. He was tough as nails, too. On paper, then, this looked to be a good team. The Bruins were about to prove it.

When this UCLA team boarded its charter and headed for Austin, a lot of fans weren't sure what to expect. It was the middle of September, and it was hot in California—and even hotter in Texas. Along with the 95-degree heat, there was plenty of good, old-fashioned Texas humidity.

UCLA coach Bob Toledo had spent several years at Texas A&M as the offensive coordinator and knew what it was like to travel to Austin and play Texas. It was never easy. Toledo never thought in a million years it would be as one-sided in favor of his UCLA Bruins as it was on Saturday, September 13, 1997, in front of 77,203 screaming Longhorns fans.

The young men from Westwood, who came into this ballgame with two straight losses to begin the season, faced a great running back in Williams, the breakaway running threat for the Longhorns. But UCLA took it to Texas right from the beginning

Coach Bob Toledo was at the helm when UCLA put together its twenty-game winning streak.
Joe Robbins

and took the fans out of the game early. In fact McNown was as hot as the Texas weather. He threw 5 touchdown passes in the first half alone without even breaking a sweat, or so it seemed. He ended the half with 202 yards in the air. McElroy caught two passes for scores, Grieb had 2 touchdown receptions, and Hicks was on the receiving end of a 43-yard scoring pass. Sailer added a 44-yard field goal and kicked all the extra points to give the Bruins a 38–0 halftime lead.

The Longhorns fans were not happy. In fact when halftime was over and the third quarter was ready to begin, half of the 77,000-plus fans had already gone home. The people left in droves. The Texas fans were hot, and it wasn't because of the weather. UCLA went on to complete a 66–3 drubbing, an amazingly one-sided victory that really started the Bruins in the right direction.

After lopsided wins over Arizona (40–27) and Houston (66–10) to run the streak to three, the Bruins got into a dogfight at Oregon. UCLA trailed at the half, 24–20, then fell behind by 11 points, much to the delight of the 42,314 Ducks fans who were as rowdy as a rugby crowd. The fans got really quiet, however, when the Bruins came from behind to win 38–31. McElroy, though suffering from a concussion, caught a 40-yard touchdown pass from McNown in the third quarter. Then McNown ran one in from a yard out to put the Bruins ahead. Chris Sailer added field goals of 56 yards (breaking the school record set in 1976 by Frank Corral) and 31 yards to ice it.

After that, the Bruins continued to roll. They beat Oregon State (34–10), California (35–17), and Stanford (27–7), to move into the AP's top ten.

Quarterback Cade McNown
breaks free from an Arizona
tackler during the second
game of the winning streak.
AP/Wide World

Against thirteenth-ranked Washington on November 15, the Rose Bowl had the feel of a New Year's Day game. There were 85,697 fans in the seats—and were they treated to something special.

In front of the big crowd, UCLA rumbled to a dominating 52–28 victory. Hicks ran for 147 yards and three scores. McNown made it look almost too easy. He had 320 yards in the air with 3 touchdown throws—one to Danny Farmer, one to McElroy, and a 67-yarder to Hicks. What an atmosphere! The victory made it eight wins in a row, and on to the last game of the regular season, against USC. UCLA had beaten its crosstown rival six consecutive years. Could the Bruins keep it up? Oh, yes, they could!

The Bruins knew that if they kept winning, they could wind up playing in the Rose Bowl on New Year's Day—as long as Washington defeated Washington State. Well, the Bruins beat USC 31–24 at the Coliseum, but the Cougars defeated the Huskies. And that was that. Washington State was headed to the Rose Bowl for the first time in sixty-seven years.

Still, the young Bruins were feeling good about themselves. They knew they let one go early in the year, up in Pullman, and that loss kept them out of the Rose Bowl. But they had just defeated USC for a record seventh straight time and had now won nine games in a row overall. Things were good. UCLA had a group of winners, and the Bruins soon received an invitation to play Texas A&M in the Cotton Bowl on New Year's Day.

When the Bruins were on their twenty-game winning streak, none were better than the ones that came against the Texas teams. Toledo had been the man who devised the offensive game plans at Texas A&M when the Aggies had some explosive teams

Hanging 10s

THE FIRST TEN: 1997 SEASON

September 13	W	66	at Texas	3
September 27	W	40	Arizona	27
October 4	W	66	Houston	10
October 11	W	39	at Oregon	31
October 18	W	34	Oregon State	10
October 25	W	35	California	17
November 1	W	27	at Stanford	7
November 15	W	52	Washington	28
November 22	W	31	at USC	24
January 1	W	29	Texas A & M (Cotton Bowl)	23

THE SECOND TEN: 1998 SEASON

September 12	W	49	Texas	31
September 19	W	42	at Houston	24
October 3	W	49	Washington State	17
October 10	W	52	at Arizona	28
October 17	W	41	Oregon	(ot) 38
October 24	W	28	at California	16
October 31	W	28	Stanford	24
November 7	W	41	at Oregon State	34
November 14	W	36	at Washington	24
November 21	W	34	USC	17

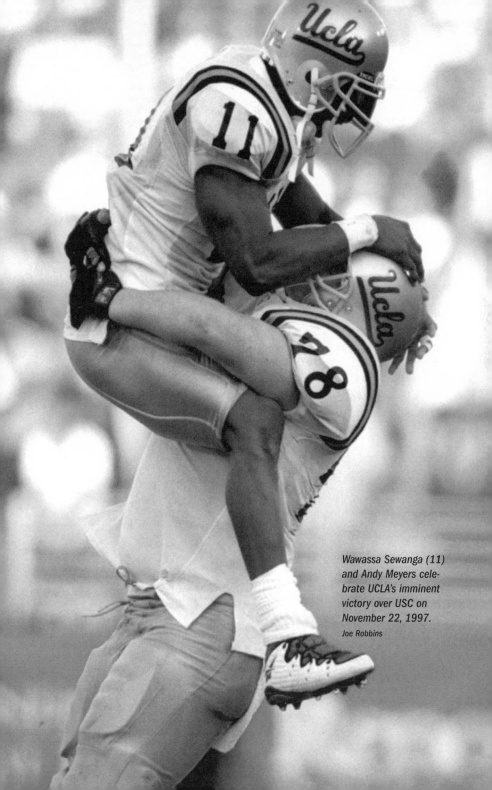

Wawassa Sewanga (11) and Andy Meyers celebrate UCLA's imminent victory over USC on November 22, 1997.
Joe Robbins

UCLA's Brian Poli-Dixon stands dejected after the Bruins win streak came to an end in Miami on December 5, 1998. AP/Wide World

and some big wins. Now he was at UCLA, in the middle of a record winning streak, and his club prepared to face his old boss's team in the Cotton Bowl in Dallas on January 1, 1998.

UCLA spotted A&M 16 points before going to work and collecting its tenth straight victory. McNown was at it again. He passed for 239 yards and 2 touchdowns, and he added another score running the football. Skip Hicks rushed for 194 yards, and the Bruins defense held the Aggies to just 247 yards. UCLA won the game, coming from behind to defeat the Aggies 29–23. The win was sweet for players and fans, but the Bruin with the biggest smile was head coach Toledo.

UCLA marched into the following season and collected ten more wins in a row. The Bruins had a couple of scares along the way. In the fifth game of the season, they beat eleventh-ranked Oregon in Pasadena, winning in overtime, 41–38, on Sailer's 24-yard field goal. It was their fifteenth straight win—the longest streak in the nation at the time.

Two weeks later, UCLA got by Stanford, 28–24, on DeShaun Foster's 8-yard touchdown run in the fourth quarter. Then the next week, at Oregon State, the Beavers kicked a late field goal to tie the Bruins at 34–34. But with just 21 seconds left in regulation, UCLA scored the winning points on a 61-yard touchdown pass from McNown to Brad Melsby. There would be two more wins, the sweetest a 34–17 rout of USC for a record eight in a row in the series and twenty straight overall. During the streak Toledo said there was no such thing as an "ugly win." And to this day, the coach is proud of the twenty-game stretch. He should be. No other UCLA coach can lay claim to that record.

The streak finally ended in Miami on December 5, 1998, when the Hurricanes earned a wild 49–45 decision. It was quite a ride while it lasted, though. An unforgettable one.

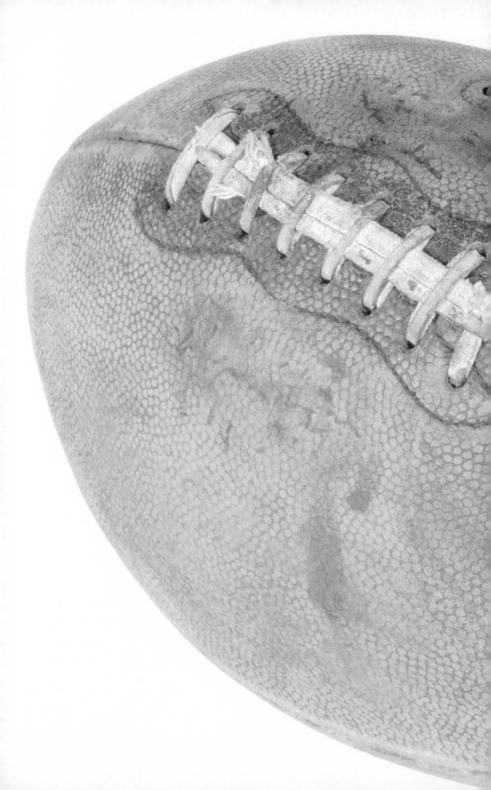

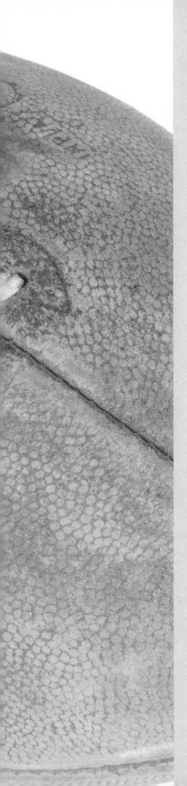

If Not for the Hurricane

The 1990s was a great decade for UCLA football. The Bruins had a terrific run of eight wins in a row against their crosstown rival, USC; collected three Pac-10 championships; had nineteen players who earned All-American honors (just about every position was represented, too); and two players, tackles Jonathan Ogden and Kris Farris, each won the Outland Trophy as college football's top interior lineman.

Early in the decade the Bruins featured two solid quarterbacks. One was Tommy Maddox, who left the school after his sophomore year in 1991 to join the Denver Broncos as a backup to future Hall of Famer John Elway. It never really worked out for Tommy in Denver, though. The young quarterback wasn't ready for the NFL, and the two years of eligibility that he gave up at UCLA were gone for good. It would be many years later that Tommy would get another shot at pro football, when he landed in Pittsburgh in 2001. That time he was ready.

When Maddox left college early, it opened the door for Wayne Cook, another talented quarterback. Cook got his chance to lead the Bruins beginning in 1992, Despite a tender knee, he put up some good numbers for the Bruins in his three seasons—throwing for 4,723 yards and 34 touchdowns in his career. In 1993 Wayne tossed 17 touchdown passes while being intercepted only four times. He also holds the record for the longest pass completion in Bruin history: 95 yards to wide receiver J. J. Stokes against Washington in 1993. Of course it was just a quick little look-in of only 5 yards—J. J. took it the final 90 yards on a fantastic run to the end zone. In 1992 quarterback John Barnes had a similar experience. He threw a 90-yard scoring pass that was also a quick little look-in to J. J. Then J. J. did the rest, running the length of the field for a dramatic touchdown to help give the Bruins a huge win over USC at the Rose Bowl.

In 1995 Cade McNown came on the scene. He started at quarterback through 1998, the year he finished third in the Heisman Trophy balloting. Cory Paus took over in 1999 and took the quarterback job into the new millennium.

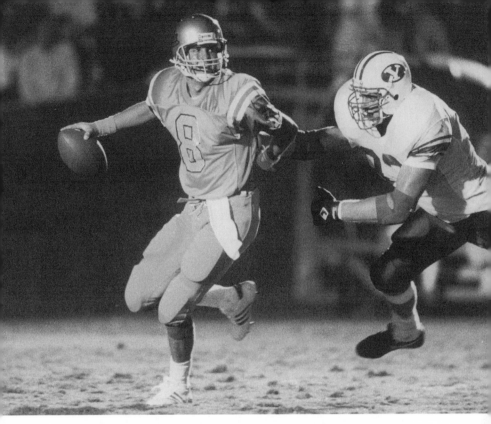

Quarterback Tommy Maddox (8) about to be sacked in a 1991 game against Brigham Young. *AP/Wide World*

There were a lot of great Bruin players from the 1990s. Two kickers who won a lot of games for the Bruins were Chris Sailer and Bjorn Merten. These guys could not only kick field goals, but punt as well. Sailer was also a kickoff specialist who could send the ball out of the end zone on a regular basis. In 1998 he extended UCLA's winning streak to fifteen games by kicking a 24-yard field goal in the second overtime at the Rose Bowl to beat Oregon 41–38.

We know what kind of a receiver J. J. Stokes was for UCLA—a school record-holder with 28 career touchdown catches. But a few other receivers stand out in the 1990s as well: Kevin Jordan, Danny Farmer, Sean LaChapelle, Jim McElroy, Brian Poli-Dixon, and Freddie Mitchell, a first-round draft choice of the Philadelphia Eagles following his junior season in 2000. Oh, yes, one more wideout who could just flat out catch: Brad Melsby. Maybe Brad didn't have the big career numbers the others did, but he sure caught some big time balls that meant a lot, especially during UCLA's twenty-game win streak in the 1997 and 1998 seasons. In particular, Bruins fans remember his big catch on the road at Oregon State in 1998. Brad caught a 61-yard touchdown strike from McNown with just 21 seconds left in the fourth quarter to give UCLA a dramatic 41–34 victory that kept the streak alive.

Kevin Jordan went on to the NFL after leaving the program in 1995 as the all-time leading receiver with 179 catches. Danny Farmer was Mr. Clutch. He came from a talented athletic family. His dad, George, was a terrific athlete at UCLA who went on to play for the NFL's Chicago Bears. In fact Danny's dad was one of the best athletes ever to come out of LaPuente High School in the San Gabriel Valley. His mom was also a great athlete. So Danny had the genes in him, and he made the most of it. Danny accumulated more receiving yards (3,020) than any other receiver in Bruins history.

Jim McElroy might have been undersized as a Division I wide receiver—he stood less than 6' and barely weighed 160 pounds—but this young man made up for his lack of size. Of all the wideouts during the 1990s, and this includes the great J. J.

Thinking Ahead

Major college football schedules are put together years in advance. Sometimes, it can be ten to twelve years ahead of time. We got an inkling that head coach Terry Donahue had his own timetable for his retirement when the Bruins announced in 1993 that they would be traveling to South Bend to play Notre Dame in 2005. Donahue was asked by a writer at his weekly press conference about playing the Irish. Terry said, "Oh, don't ask me, I'll be long gone by then, retired. You'll have to ask the new guy, whoever it is, that question." In 1995 Donahue did retire as the winningest coach in Pac-10 history.

Stokes, nobody had better separation from a defender when the ball was in the air than McElroy. That was his specialty. Throw the ball up there, and if Jim was stride for stride with the defender, he would leave the opposing player in the dust and catch the football. Jimmy was also tough. He would take a big hit and jump up like nothing happened. It was unreal. Wow, was he fun to watch!

The defensive backs were excellent, beginning with Eric Turner, Matt Darby, Carlton Gray, Marvin Goodwin, Larry Atkins, Shaun Williams, and Tommy Bennett. These guys were not only ball hawks, but they also would come up and hit in run-support situations, making it easier for linemen and linebackers to be active in the defensive scheme.

Jonathan Ogden was a tackle who won the Outland Trophy in 1995. The next spring, he was selected in the first round of the NFL draft by the Baltimore Ravens. Tackle Kris Farris won the award in 1998, then was drafted in the third round by the Pittsburgh Steelers. Ogden and Farris were two of the best offensive linemen in college football in the 1990s. Other outstanding linemen at UCLA included guys like Chad Overhauser, Craig Novitsky, Vaughn Parker, Mike Flanagan, and Andy Meyers—players up front who not only were great blockers but were leaders on the field as well. Those guys made the offense go!

Look, you can argue that a man like Ogden, who stands 6' 9" and weighs 345 pounds, should be able to block well, but what is really amazing is how these 300-pound guys can move! They are fast, agile, and quick. That is what sets them apart from the average big man walking the streets. And what about the little defensive back who might be 5' 10" inches tall and weigh 185 pounds? He not only has to be able to defend the great pass receivers who are bigger than him, but he also has to fight off those big linemen who are downfield on rushing plays, then try to make a tackle on a running back who could be 225 or 250 pounds or more. A football team is an ensemble of special people of all shapes and sizes. These players have a talent that most of us can only dream about.

Center Mike Flanagan is quite a story, although not that unusual at a school like UCLA. Some years you have more talent at one position than another. But most of the time there's quite a bit of depth on both sides of the football. As a sophomore in 1993, Mike was just a reserve lineman. He didn't really impress anyone, but did his job as a solid backup. Then he got a chance to play at Stanford against the Cardinal and really started to show his worth.

Jonathan Ogden (right) holds a Baltimore Ravens jacket after being selected in the first round of the NFL draft in 1996. *AP/Wide World*

He not only impressed his teammates, but he also graded out well on video in front of his coaches. They found out that Mike was a gamer. He was the kind of a player who didn't really wow people at practice, but during the game—look out! He could play. After that Stanford game, he played in every game until he graduated and was drafted by the Green Bay Packers.

Two linebackers from the 1990s who could make a big difference in a defensive game plan were Roman Phifer and Jamir Miller. Roman has shown his staying power in the NFL since UCLA. Jamir could dominate a collegiate game to the point that if he wasn't playing, some of the Bruin faithful (including coaches) felt they were at a big disadvantage without him.

Bob Toledo took pride in putting points on the board, first as an offensive coordinator for head coach Terry Donahue and then running his own show as coach in the mid-1990s. His teams featured some wide-open passing offenses and an assortment of trick plays. But Bob was the first to say that the rushing game had to be there, too. And, man alive, did he and Donahue have rushers! Skip Hicks could run with the best of them. So could Karim Abdul-Jabbar. Both went over a thousand yards in a season, and both did it two times! Kevin Williams did it in 1991. And DeShaun Foster got into the act near the end of the 1990s and put his mark on the program in 2000 with 1,037 yards rushing for the year.

The Bruins had a legitimate shot at playing for the national title during the 1990s. It all came down to the Hurricane Bowl of 1998. It wasn't really a bowl game, of course. It was just called that by sportswriters and fans, because the game had been postponed on account of Hurricane Georges. Many people feel the Bruins would probably have won this game if it had been played

*Running back
DeShaun Foster
looks for an opening
in a game against
Stanford in 2000.*
AP/Wide World

at its regular time. But Hurricane Georges had other ideas, and the Bruins were upended by Miami 49–45.

The game originally had been scheduled for September 26 and finally took place in December. The ensuing loss was more than just another defeat. Not only did it end the Bruins amazing twenty-game winning streak, but if the Bruins had beaten Miami, they likely would have played the University of Tennessee in the Fiesta Bowl for the national title. But, of course, that didn't happen.

The Bruins certainly scored enough points to win. But they just couldn't stop Miami's offense. Edgerrin James was a young running back who rushed for 299 yards against the Bruins. The defense that day was not at its best, that's for sure. But Mr. James made a name for himself. He not only starred in that game, but he also would eventually prove to be a terrific rusher for the NFL's Indianapolis Colts.

Quarterback Cade McNown tried his best to keep the Bruins in the game. He passed for 513 yards, including 5 touchdown strikes, but it wasn't enough to stop the Hurricanes. Oh, but for Hurricane Georges, who knows what would've happened?

Some people feel as though the football program under Toledo never recovered from that nightmare in Miami. That might not be a fair assessment. Other factors always enter in. For instance, many observers late in the 1990s thought that the Bruins future was in a young quarterback by the name of J. P. Losman. When Losman came to UCLA, part of the agreement was that Toledo wouldn't recruit any other young quarterbacks from Losman's high-school graduating class. A young man by the name of Kyle Boller from Hart High School in nearby Newhall,

California, wanted to be a Bruin in the worst way, but he was from the same class as J. P. So Toledo didn't actively pursue Boller. When Losman left, Boller had already committed to Pac-10 rival California. Toledo didn't get either young quarterback to play for him. Boller went on to become a star at California and was a first-round draft choice of the Baltimore Ravens in 2003. Losman transferred to Tulane and was drafted by the Buffalo Bills in the first round in 2004.

The Quarterback Club

There is an old saying that a quarterback is overrated until you don't have one. Or he gets too much of the credit when a football team wins and too much of the blame when the team loses. One thing for sure, though, is that a quarterback is an integral part of any team. A good one can literally carry a club with his arm. And a poor one can make a great team look mediocre.

It used to be that quarterbacks called all their own plays. That has changed over the years. Now it doesn't matter if it's youth football or the NFL, almost all plays are called from the sidelines by the coaching staff. Good signal callers do have the ability to change the play at the line of scrimmage. This in itself is an art. Some players never master it. Other players practice it and are adequate. And some are just flat out great—though the ones who rise above the others are few and far between.

It's like coaches calling pitches from the dugout in a baseball game. Catchers and pitchers were once the only ones who made the decision on what was to be thrown. Some still do. But by and large, most pitches come from the bench, just like football plays come from the sideline. The bottom line is that coaches and their staffs are more involved than ever before in the play calling for both offense and defense. Execution is now the most important factor in playing quarterback.

And that raises an interesting question: Is it fair to compare quarterbacks from one era to another? Oh, sure, you can look at numbers and see what an individual has done over the course of a season or a career. But sometimes numbers can be misleading. The late Jim Healey, our old broadcasting pal from the original KMPC days, told anyone who would listen that the best quarterback of all time was Bob Waterfield. For his era Waterfield was fantastic. It was the early 1940s when Waterfield played at UCLA. And yet he is still in the record books as the number fifteen passer in school history. That is remarkable in this day and age of inflated offensive numbers.

Cory Paus, who finished his collegiate career in 2002, is ranked number two on the Bruins all-time passing list. Is he the second-best passer ever to attend UCLA? Believe me, Cory had a nice career. But there are more factors that go into ranking quarterbacks than numbers alone.

For instance Paul Cameron, who played halfback in the Single Wing for Red Sanders from 1951 to 1953, is listed in the school record books as one of the top passers and one of the all-time leaders in total offense because in his era he would run the ball, not just pass. Billy Kilmer was another halfback in head coach Bill Barnes's Single Wing who is one of the all-time leaders in total offense. Both Cameron and Kilmer were All-Americans. They were among the best players UCLA ever produced.

There have been only two more Bruin passers to reach All-America status since then: Troy Aikman and Cade McNown. There are some fans who feel Aikman might be the overall best to come out of UCLA, especially when they include his three Super Bowl championships in the NFL. Others say McNown was the best, not only because of his superlative numbers, but also because of a career that included twenty straight victories his last two years.

You will never get Terry Donahue, the winningest coach in Pac-10 history, to say whom he thinks is the best UCLA quarterback. "We had so many great players who could pass the ball it would be unfair to say who's the best," Donahue said. But he does admit that "Troy Aikman was the most accurate passer of all the ones I coached at UCLA."

Really there are several quarterbacks who may not have achieved All-America status but who were solid players for UCLA. One who stands out is Tom Ramsey. "We've had some good ones," Donahue said. "They were all different but good, and Tom is right up there with the best of the best."

Best of the Best

The year of the quarterback in the NFL draft was 1983. John Elway, Todd Blackledge, Tony Eason, Jim Kelly, Dan Marino, and Ken O'Brien were all first-round draft picks coming out of college. But it was UCLA's Tom Ramsey who led all quarterbacks in passing efficiency the previous fall with an NCAA-record rating of 153.5 (Ramsey also set the career record of 143.9). He was selected in the 10th round in 1983 by the New England Patriots.

Ramsey's collegiate career spanned from 1979 to 1982, and for years he ranked as UCLA's all-time leader in passing, total offense, and touchdown passes. He started a couple of games as a freshman before taking over the reigns as Donahue's quarterback in his sophomore year. He never had to look over his shoulder again.

Ramsey talks about the brotherhood of UCLA quarterbacks as something special. He looked up to John Sciarra and Mark Harmon, who preceded him. And he would pass on that sentiment to the guys he competed with, like Steve Bono, Rick Neuheisel, and Rick Bashore, and to others who followed him at the position, like David Norrie, Matt Stevens, Aikman, and Tommy Maddox. "We all knew each other and we all pulled for one another," Stevens said. "Sure, you wanted to always be the starter but, sometimes when it didn't work out you pulled like crazy for the other guy because you just wanted to win."

When Ramsey got to UCLA, he watched a team transform from the veer offense to a more wide-open passing game. It was the time of the quarterback. John Elway was graduating from high school at the same time as Ramsey and they would be competing in the Pac-10, Ramsey as a Bruin and Elway at Stanford. Terry Donahue brought in Homer Smith as UCLA's offensive coordinator and made a full commitment to, as Ramsey called it, "the West Coast style of offense." UCLA recruited players who could throw the ball downfield and, of course, there was more pressure on the quarterback to perform for the team to be successful.

Quarterback Tom Ramsey goes down low against Michigan in the Rose Bowl on January 1, 1983. AP/Wide World

One of the great things about the quarterback club at UCLA was that every one of the players had his day in the sun. "We all had our respective bowl games," Ramsey said. "I had the Rose Bowl in 1983 [UCLA beat Michigan 24–14], Neuheisel had the Rose Bowl in 1984 [a 45–9 victory over Illinois], Bono had the Fiesta Bowl [the Bruins beat Miami 39–37 in the 1985 game], and Norrie and Stevens had the 1986 Rose Bowl [when UCLA defeated the favored Iowa Hawkeyes 45–28]."

Ramsey felt the icing on the cake was when the Dallas Cowboys made Aikman the number one overall choice in the 1989 NFL draft. "It made all of us quarterbacks feel good about ourselves," Ramsey said. They had one of their own picked tops at their position.

Ramsey was one of the fortunate ones who had the ability to start as a freshman. Now, it might have been only two games, but that early playing time fueled the fire for his next three seasons as the Bruins quarterback. Just the experience of getting ready for a game as a young UCLA signal caller paid some big dividends later.

During this time Ramsey felt he really grew as a football player and as a young man. It all came to fruition in 1980. That was when the Bruins made a concerted effort to move the ball in the passing game. But by the same token, they knew they had to run the ball and play good defense, too, in order to be a successful team. Running back Freeman McNeil had his coming-out party that year. It was also the era of safety Kenny Easley. He was Mr. Defense, a linebacker playing defensive back. Oh, could he hit!

As far as Ramsey was concerned, McNeil and Easley were the best examples of senior leadership on the team. He felt he learned more about guidance and direction from those two men than from any others. So, when it was Ramsey's turn to be the one in charge, he was ready. His 1982 team made an impact that carried right through the decade. It gave the teams that followed something to live up to, and they did.

Players such as Karl Morgan, Irv Eatman, Cormac Carney, Jo Jo Townsell, and Tom Sullivan, just to name a few, came into the program during Ramsey's years and had a major impact on how to play UCLA football. They passed it on to the new recruits who would become Bruins. Morgan, Sullivan, and Ramsey were tri-captains their senior year. In addition Donahue had superb continuity on his coaching staff that maximized the talent of his ball club. That was one of Donahue's strengths. He could evaluate talent, whether it was a player or—sometimes more importantly—one of his coaches.

Ramsey grew up in the San Fernando Valley and was turned on to football at a very young age. He was only nine when he played for the North Valley Golden Bears. His young days were blessed with good coaches and good teams that won often, including championships. In other words, Ramsey got used to winning. His brother Dave played on some teams that weren't as well coached and didn't have some of the most talented players. Those teams weren't as successful. Within the same family, they experienced winning and losing. And, as coaches love to say, either one can become a habit.

Ramsey eventually became a three-year starter at Kennedy High School and played in the same league as John Elway, who was at Granada Hills High School. San Fernando Valley high schools had produced their share of stars such as Anthony Davis, Kenny and Malcolm Moore, and Kevin Williams, who would go on to play at Southern California. During the mid- and late 1970s, there was a lot of scouting attention focused on this particular area of greater Los Angeles.

Ramsey remembers going to a UCLA game when the Bruins played California while he was in high school. He watched Theotis Brown run over the Bears' players all day, then went into the locker room afterwards and was struck by the players singing the fight song and by the strong camaraderie of the team. Ramsey later said, "I thought, this is a pretty good spot." He meant UCLA football. (The tradition of singing the fight song after a Bruins victory is still alive.)

Ramsey's first inclination had been to go out of state to college, and why not? He was recruited by Notre Dame, Washington, Arizona, and Oregon State. The Beavers were the only school that said he would start the first game of the season his freshman year. When Ramsey looked at the Oregon State schedule for the following season, he noticed that the Trojans were game two and just coming off a national championship. He told his parents, "It might not be the best thing to end up in a body cast the second week of the season my freshman year." The opportunity to play was something that Ramsey felt he had to earn, anyway. He would do that at UCLA, and he would make the most of it.

Ramsey originally was both a baseball player and a football player in high school. He was a catcher in baseball and was pretty good. He could hit, had a great arm, and liked running the ball club from behind the dish. He was an all-star in Little League, Pony League, and Colt League baseball, but he had to make a decision after his freshman year at Kennedy, and he decided to go with football. He became a three-year starter in high school and never second-guessed his decision, especially when he started getting letters from college recruiters after his sophomore year. He really got bombarded with correspondence after his team went to the city semifinals his junior season.

Ramsey's high school coaches—head coach John Haynes and assistants Jim Babcock and Dick Whitney—became mentors and good friends with whom he still keeps in touch to this day. They all had a tremendous influence on him.

Coach Haynes had a wide-open offense that would throw thirty times a game. He had a sophisticated offensive scheme that many colleges don't even run. But he still believed in having a running game based around all that passing. It was quarterback heaven for Ramsey. He learned the fundamentals of pass routes and combination routes and how to read defenses. "I used to sit in game-planning meetings with the coaching staff in high school when I was a junior and senior," Ramsey said. Those opportunities did nothing but help in his preparation for college football.

Wide receiver Willie Curran was the host recruiting player who got Ramsey excited about playing for the Bruins. "He was your typical California guy," Ramsey said. "Surfer, loved the ocean. He was fast as lightning, worked hard, and was an excellent student."

Curran showed Ramsey the ropes. He introduced him to campus and life at UCLA. He showed the young quarterback that he could live on campus, off campus, commute, keep a low profile if he wished—really do what made him most comfortable. Curran also made it very clear that Bruin football functioned as

Center Dan Dufour (59) lifts tailback Danny Andrews after Andrews scored in the January 1983 Rose Bowl. AP/Wide World

an extended family. Ramsey liked that more than anything else. Who needed a frat house? The football team would be Ramsey's fraternity.

In the beginning, like many other young college freshmen, Ramsey was lukewarm about staying local and not leaving the state to play college football. But by the time his sophomore season rolled around, he knew he had made the right decision. Ramsey felt that everyone on the ball club was pulling in the right direction and that the Bruins could compete for a championship.

The first time Ramsey got a chance to play his freshman year was against twentieth-ranked Washington in the eighth game of the season. On his first series he called an audible and threw a corner route to Jo Jo Townsell for a touchdown. "We have a young kid who can make plays," Donahue thought. That was just the beginning.

Eventually, Ramsey passed for 6,168 yards and 50 touchdowns in his collegiate career. He completed 62 percent of his passes for 2,986 yards and 21 touchdowns as a senior in 1982. And with Ramsey at the helm, UCLA finished the 1980 season ranked fifth in the nation, went to the Bluebonnet Bowl in 1981, and won the Rose Bowl to close the 1982 season. Ramsey capped his career by earning the Rose Bowl's player-of-the-game award in UCLA's victory over Michigan on New Year's Day 1983.

One thing that was always very apparent about Ramsey is how confident he was. And yet, he has always portrayed himself humbly. "I was a little more brazen," he said about his early years as a Bruin, "because of my background in high school and being so involved in the offense. I loved to get after it and compete on the field and was able to do that because of the people around

From Scout Team to Team Star

Tom Ramsey remembers a scrawny blond-headed kid whose locker was next to his. His name was Rick Neuheisel, a walk-on who would be the scout-team quarterback and get beat up, dirtied, and bloodied by Kenny Easley and the rest of the first-team defense on a daily basis. Meanwhile, "Rams," as Tom's teammates called him, felt guilty at times because he would never be touched in practice as the first-team quarterback. But when Neuheisel got his chance, he would eventually earn a football scholarship and be a Rose Bowl MVP. That in particular made Ramsey feel good, because Neuheisel truly earned it.

me. I had both good players and good coaches. That's the great game of football."

Guts might be what coaches would call Ramsey's brazenness. He always thought he could get it done. He never let anyone or anybody tell him different. One aspect of his career that he never dwelled on was his size. He was listed at 6' 1" and 185 pounds. He played at about the same size for eight years professionally, maybe a little heavier. But that was it. He never let anyone tell him that a 6' 4" or 6' 5" quarterback at 230 pounds was going to be better than him. He just dismissed things that he felt were irrelevant and moved on. He just got the job done, period.

He says the accomplishment he is most proud of is being selected to the UCLA Hall of Fame. "You have a wonderful sense of satisfaction because you travel this road of success, and successful teams just don't happen," he said. "It is a whole combination of players pulling together, the equipment staff, the trainers, the leadership in the locker room, the coaching staff and their leadership, and the game planning. Even the fan base is important." Spoken like a true winner.

Past Perfect, Future Bright

It is truly amazing that UCLA, with its late start as an institution of higher learning, has come as far as it has in such a short time. Don't get me wrong, 1919 (the year that UCLA was founded) was quite a long time ago—just not such a long time for a university that has been as successful as the Westwood campus. Who would have thought that two men in 1915 could put together an idea for a new college in young Los Angeles and turn it into one of the most respected campuses in the world in fewer than one hundred years? The UCLA insignia is one of the most sought after around the globe. There are stories of people traveling abroad being offered large sums of money for a UCLA windbreaker, shirt, hat, or uniform.

Moving the little school from Vermont Avenue in Los Angeles to Westwood was a stroke of genius. Who would have thought that the campus would be in the midst of some of the most prime property in southern California, or that students from all over the world would relish being accepted into this great university?

Fred Cozens, the first head football coach and athletic director, had no idea what kind of program he was establishing or the journey on which he was embarking. He probably was just trying to get through those early years after the end of World War I the best he could.

The new university was just trying to survive. As the years rolled along, the foundation for success was put in place. It took time, but it happened—the school succeeded both academically and in intercollegiate athletics.

Athletic director Dan Guerrero was asked if he ever looks to the past to see the future. He said, "Oh, very much so." He also borrowed a line from President Harry Truman and said, "'The only thing that is new in this world is the history we don't know.'

"What is so applicable to our situation, relative to the Truman quote," Guerrero went on to say, "is that when you look at the great coaches who have been at UCLA—not just head coaches but assistants as well—the great athletes on both sides of the ball and what they have accomplished, there is no question that the successes of the past have a bearing on what might be possible for the future."

The UCLA Marching Band is one of the finest in the land. Joe Robbins

UCLA has made great strides in football over the years. Head coaches of the past left their mark on the program that later gridiron leaders looked back on and drew inspiration from. It took some time, but the program gained respect back in the 1920s, when William Spaulding came to town. "Babe" Horrell continued the tradition into the 1940s, along with Bert LaBrucherie. Then the program really took off with the hiring of Red Sanders in 1949. The era of the 1950s belonged to Sanders. Red died way too young. Who knows what kind of legacy he would have left if he could have lived just into his sixties? The nine years he was at the football helm were special.

Terry Donahue said that the past made him a better coach for the future during his tenure. Of course he also played at

UCLA, which had an effect on him as a coach, but he was never afraid to embrace the coaches who preceded him. In fact, Donahue promoted the past as almost legendary to his players. He got them to realize they had a responsibility to the tradition of UCLA football.

Think about it: The tradition started on old Moore Field, back when the campus was on Vermont Avenue. A lot of blood, sweat, and—you better believe—tears went into the early years of the program, whether the Bruins won or lost games.

Isn't that what the future is all about? Looking to the past and being proud of what has taken place. Donahue was perhaps best at it among UCLA's coaches. He urged his players to be accountable, to be responsible for their own duties when they practiced and, especially, when they hit the playing field on game day. Because, he'd stress, they were making history.

It was so moving to see the players who won the 1954 national championship come back in 2004 to celebrate the fiftieth anniversary of that great season. To see them being introduced at halftime of the homecoming game against Stanford was inspirational. Could that be the reason UCLA played so well and shut out the Cardinal that day?

The one thing Guerrero is trying to instill in all Bruin athletes is pride in UCLA's tradition. As a former second baseman for the Bruins baseball team (he's in the school's baseball hall of fame), he continues to build on that foundation of success. UCLA has it, so why not continue to be proud of it, and to remember it?

The Bruins football team plays its games in the Rose Bowl. It is hallowed ground, where the Tournament of Roses game is

The UCLA Philosophy

"If we are not moving forward, we're losing ground," says athletic director Dan Guerrero. "The UCLA philosophy is to build a nationally competitive program with quality student-athletes who not only can compete at the highest level in the country on the gridiron, but also compete with the finest students in America in the classroom."

played every year. Everyone knows that when you think Rose Bowl, you think not only of New Year's Day but also the home of UCLA. "We're proud of that," Guerrero said.

It is inspiring when former football greats, such as linebackers Donn Moomaw and Jerry Robinson, stroll onto the field at home games for the toss of the coin. Current players watching experience a tremendous example of the eyes of the future looking into the eyes of the past. Is there any better tradition than that? It's the best. The players, the great wins, the Rose Bowl victories, the wonderful upsets—all of these things are part of the Bruin lore that lives on forever.

Guerrero is very proud of the nine national championships UCLA has won in various sports since he took over as the head of the athletic department in 2002. UCLA's ninety-five national titles in all through 2004 is an intercollegiate record. Not bad for a young university. There are plenty of other schools a lot older that cannot even come close to such numbers.

Head coach Karl Dorrell shouts instructions to his team during a game in 2004.
AP/Wide World

Karl Dorrell was hired as head football coach in December 2002 to carry on the great gridiron tradition at UCLA. The fifteenth coach in the history of the program knows all about the Bruins tradition because he played football for the university. Like Guerrero, they know what it is like to represent the school on the playing field.

Dorrell's first season started out great. Heading into November the Bruins were 6–2 with five straight wins, including four in a row against Pac-10 opponents. But UCLA closed out the year with five tough losses. That only made Dorrell more determined about the future—it had to improve. He was emphatic that his team would get better. Hard work in the weight room, off-season conditioning, recruiting—all were issues that his team had to address. They did, and it paid off in 2004.

The spring of 2004 had an air of newness. It also had the feel of experience. At the traditional spring game, you could see the growth immediately. That's the way the coach wanted it to be. It was development and maturation rolled into one. Some key changes on the coaching staff also were evident. Offensive coordinator Tom Cable, quarterbacks coach Jim Svoboda, and wide receivers coach Dino Babers were added to the staff.

The players could feel it, too. They were comfortable with the second year under this regime. They knew the system better, and they knew what was expected of them. You could sense their confidence. Experience is a funny thing. When you combine it with hard work and a positive outlook, there is only one way to go, and that's forward. That is what Dorrell was looking for.

UCLA started the 2004 season by winning four of its first five games. It could have been 5–0, but in the opening game of the year at the Rose Bowl, the team made four critical turnovers that sealed its fate. The Bruins lost 31–20 to Oklahoma State.

Of course, "coulda, woulda, shoulda" doesn't work in college football. When you make that many mistakes, it's hard to win. But looking back, the Oklahoma State game was winnable. Cowboys running back Vernand Morency rushed for 261 yards. It diminished two running touchdowns from Manuel White, including a 60-yard dash, the longest of his career.

The previous year Dave and Matt Ball were bookend defensive ends. The two defensive tackles were Ryan Boscetti and Rodney Leisle. All were seniors in 2003, so they were gone. The 2004 defensive line was young and inexperienced. It was evident right from the first game: UCLA had trouble stopping the run.

It wasn't as if the Bruins weren't trying. They were green and untrained on the Division I level. They needed playing time. Of the eleven to twelve defensive lineman who would play on a rotating basis, there were only one senior and two juniors. The rest were sophomores and redshirt freshmen or true freshmen. They would get playing time, and yardage given up would be the price to pay. Some of those new young men on the block did open some eyes, though. True freshman Brigham Harwell was one. The coaches call his gift "quick feet."

After dropping the opener to Oklahoma State, UCLA went on a four-game winning streak. The Bruins hit the road first to get it underway. Illinois was the first victim, in Champaign. The Bruins Maurice Drew ran for 142 yards and a touchdown, while quarterback Drew Olson tossed three scoring passes, two to Craig Bragg and one to tight end Marcedes Lewis in a 35–17 win. White had 97 yards rushing.

The University of Washington was next. For the second week in a row, the Bruins were on the road. They beat the Huskies 37–31. Maurice Drew rushed for 322 yards, a new school record, and five scores. What a game! The Bruins had to gang-tackle Huskies receiver Charles Fredrick at the 2 yard line as time ran out to secure the win.

UCLA returned to Pasadena and beat up on San Diego State 33–10. Drew again had a good day, running the football for

Even the coaches get into the cheering at UCLA's games.
Joe Robbins

161 yards and a touchdown. Olson teamed with Tab Perry on a 65-yard touchdown pass, and linebacker Spencer Havner, a tackling machine, intercepted a pass and ran it back to the end zone from 52 yards out. All-Pac-10 kicker Justin Medlock kicked four field goals.

The fourth win in a row was a 37–17 victory over Arizona. It was a breakout game for Lewis, who caught three touchdown passes and made some great grabs to keep drives alive in the win. Olson established a new career high with four touchdown throws. Chris Horton blocked a punt for the first score of the day.

While hitting the road again for Berkeley, the Bruins knew the next game would be tough. Playing in Strawberry Canyon against the Bears, they lost 45–28. Aaron Rodgers may have been the best quarterback the Bruins faced all year. He tossed four touchdown passes in the Bears win, while the Bruins Olson had four himself. UCLA had a chance in the first half, when they battled back to tie the game at 14–14, but it was all Bears in the second half. They finished with 558 yards total offense.

There isn't anyone associated with the Bruins program who doesn't agree that the next game at Arizona State was one that got away. Turnovers were a killer. After leading by 11 points with 7:12 left, the Bruins lost 45–42. Sun Devils quarterback Andrew Walter tossed six touchdown passes and threw for 419 yards. UCLA's Drew Olson had two touchdown passes but also four critical interceptions. The Bruins got rushing performances of 81 yards from White, 62 yards from Drew, and 80 yards from true freshman Chris Markey (on just five carries). It was a very tough loss.

A funny thing happened, though. The Bruins didn't let the rough outing in Tempe get to them. Sometimes those kinds of

"We're Number One!"

UCLA is proud to be number one in the country in NCAA championships across all athletic competition. "When you are looking for success, every place has a formula that works," says athletic director Dan Guerrero. "The formula that works at UCLA is a great academic institution, great location, fabulous coaches, a true commitment to excel, and now a tradition and legacy that is second to none."

losses can devastate a team for the remainder of a schedule. Not this ball club. Olson called it his best game. He wasn't about to let the loss ruin his season. He knew the interceptions were bad, but he vowed to keep going. You've got to hand it to the junior quarterback: His intestinal fortitude was amazing.

Coach Dorrell was the same way. He said his ball club was going to look forward to playing Stanford the upcoming weekend and to enjoy Homecoming. Not that the loss didn't hurt, but the Bruins were moving forward. It would make them even stronger.

The Bruins handed Stanford a big goose egg. They shut out the Cardinal 21–0 and really did put the loss in Tempe behind them. A defense that had been under attack all season for not stopping the running game and giving up lots of yardage shut down Stanford's offense completely. It was a huge win for Dorrell and the program.

The "Man Train," Manuel White, rushed for 87 yards and a touchdown on 12 carries. Drew rushed 12 times for 105 yards; he also caught a TD pass from Olson on a beautiful misdirection play at the goal line. Plus, little Maurice added a spectacular 68-yard punt return for a touchdown. Was this the same team from a week ago? They felt they could beat anyone now.

But hold everything—the Washington State Cougars were coming to town. The Bruins were favored to win and, just when you thought the coast was clear, "Wazoo" and a running back returning to Pasadena had other ideas. A young man named Jerome Harrison, who had played at Pasadena City College before transferring to Pullman, had the game of his life against the Bruins. He rushed for 247 yards and 3 touchdowns.

The Bruins made a major mistake by losing the ball on the opening kickoff. "It's bad luck to fumble the opening kickoff," said my broadcasting partner Matt Stevens.

UCLA played catch-up to the Cougars the entire afternoon and lost 31–29. It was another game that the Bruins felt got away from them. They did battle back from a 31–16 deficit with two touchdown throws from Olson to Tab Perry (who had fumbled that kickoff) and another to White. But a two-point conversion try to tie the game late in the fourth quarter was unsuccessful. It was another heartbreaker.

UCLA had two tough opponents left, and they needed one win to become bowl eligible. First up was a road game in Eugene against Oregon, followed by the last game of the regular season against the number one team in the country, crosstown rival USC.

The Bruins were resilient. They shook off the loss to Washington State like a bad habit. The players and coaching staff went into Autzen Stadium knowing they had to take the crowd out of the game, and they did it. The Bruins won 34–26.

Markey, a true freshman, had a great game. The Luling, Louisiana, native rushed for 131 yards and caught 5 passes for 84 more, for a total of 215 yards from scrimmage. White added 82 yards and two touchdowns rushing, while Medlock became the first Bruin to kick two field goals from 50 or more yards in the same game. One was from 52 and the other was from an even 50 to ice the game. UCLA was bowl bound.

But first it was USC at home after a three-week layoff. "Why a three-week bye?" everyone asked. ABC Television, that's why. The network wanted a showcase game to go against some of the conference championship games around the country. The folks at ABC ponied up the money, and both schools said yes. So, that's how it came about.

UCLA's rivalry with USC remains one of the biggest in the NCAA. Joe Robbins

UCLA fans let the world know whom they think is number one. *Joe Robbins*

The Trojans went into the contest as 23-point favorites. The Bruins not only played them tough, they also had a shot at winning late in the game. USC won 29–24. UCLA actually outscored the Trojans 14–9 in the second half. The highly touted number one team in the country, which had made major adjustments to their opponents all year at halftime, could not figure out UCLA in the final thirty minutes on both offense and defense.

USC quarterback Matt Leinart, the eventual Heisman Trophy winner, did not throw a touchdown pass for the first time in twenty-five games. Reggie Bush, another Heisman finalist, had good numbers but fumbled twice, the last one setting up the Bruins last chance. But an interception ended UCLA's upset hopes, and the Trojans ran out the clock.

"I'm proud of the fact that our coaching staff overcame some great odds," Guerrero said. "There was new air breathed into this program. The players and coaches did it with the class and the character that I knew they would, and they did it in a manner that was reflective of this great institution. They did it in a very positive and distinctive fashion. We are clearly not back to where we want to be, but we're gaining on it very, very quickly. The future looks bright down the road."

No one can predict what will happen in the future. That's what makes it so much fun, and as the old saying goes, "That's why they play the games." But we know one thing: The Bruin tradition will live on. It always has.

THE INSIDER'S SOURCE

With more than 540 West-related titles, we have the area covered. Whether you're looking for the path less traveled, a favorite place to eat, family-friendly fun, a breathtaking hike, or enchanting local attractions, our pages are filled with ideas to get you from one state to the next.

For a complete listing of all our titles, please visit our Web site at www.GlobePequot.com. The Globe Pequot Press is the largest publisher of local travel books in the United States and is a leading source for outdoor recreation guides.

FOR BOOKS TO THE WEST

INSIDERS' GUIDE®

FALCON GUIDE®

Available wherever books are sold.
Orders can also be placed on the Web at www.GlobePequot.com,
by phone from 8:00 A.M. to 5:00 P.M. at 1-800-243-0495,
or by fax at 1-800-820-2329.